Franz Schönfellner

Krems schafft Zukunft
Krems creates the Future

LWmedia

Franz Schönfellner

Krems schafft Zukunft

Medieninhaber:
LW Werbe- und Verlags GmbH, www.lwmedia.at, Krems-Wien
Herausgeber: Erwin Goldfuss
Geschäftsleitung: Claudia Altrichter
Redaktion: Franz Schönfellner
Fotos: Manuel Tauber-Romieri
Kreation: Fritz Gillinger
Grafik: Christina Plener
Übersetzung: Wordworks, Neil Perkins
Druck: Druckerei Janetschek GmbH

ISBN 978-3-9504163-3-6

UNIVERSUM MAGAZIN

KREMS

SCHAFFT ZUKUNFT
CREATES THE FUTURE

FRANZ SCHÖNFELLNER
MIT FOTOS VON MANUEL TAUBER-ROMIERI

INHALT
CONTENTS

Franz Schönfellner, geboren 1955 in Krems, ist Kulturhistoriker und Autor. Er hat als Wissenschaftler und als langjähriger Mitarbeiter und Leiter der Kultur- und Bildungsabteilung sowie des Museums der Stadt Krems zahlreiche Publikationen, Bücher und Vorträge gestaltet und geschrieben.

Franz Schönfellner, *cultural historian and author, was born in Krems in 1955. He has worked for many years for, and been head of, the Department of Culture and Education and the Krems Municipal Museum. In this capacity he has written and been responsible for many publications, books and lectures.*

Manuel Tauber-Romieri, geboren 1987, lebt als freischaffender Fotograf und Medienkünstler in St. Pölten und ist bekannt durch eine Vielzahl von Arbeiten für Magazine, Zeitschriften, Publikationen und Agenturen. Ausstellungen seiner künstlerischen Arbeiten begleiten seinen erfolgreichen Weg.
www.manueltauberromieri.com

Manuel Tauber-Romieri, *born in 1987, lives as a freelance photographer and media artist in St. Pölten and is known for his numerous contributions to magazines, publications and agencies. Exhibitions of his work provide proof of his success as an artist.*
www.manueltauberromieri.com

Aus der mittelalterlichen Handels- und Weinstadt am Ausgang der Wachau wurde in den letzten Jahrzehnten eine pulsierende Kultur- und Bildungsstadt mit enormem Potenzial für die Zukunft. Die Altstädte von Krems und von Stein haben Weltkulturerbestatus, im Osten davon forscht und wächst die Industrie. Im Westen, im Stadtteil Stein, gedeihen Bildungseinrichtungen von internationalem Format. Eingebettet in die Weinberge, bietet Krems auch dank der mittlerweile viel beachteten Kulturangebote hohe Lebensqualität. Und ob der optimalen Lage dazu kurze Wege wie kaum eine vergleichbare Stadt.

In recent decades, the medieval trade and wine-growing city at the gateway to the Wachau valley has become a vibrant city of culture and education with enormous potential. The historic centres of Krems and Stein are World Heritage Sites. To the east, industry conducts research and expands. In the western district of Stein, educational institutions of international stature are thriving. Nestling amid the vineyards, Krems provides a high quality of life, not least thanks to its cultural activities which have gained widespread recognition. And its ideal location means distances are shorter than in almost any comparable town.

PRÄDIKAT: AUSGEZEICHNET
RATING: EXCELLENT

Krems an der Donau ist eine der lebenswertesten Städte Österreichs. Das wird immer wieder aufs Neue bestätigt. Nicht zuletzt durch hunderttausende Touristen, die die Schönheit des Weltkulturerbes Wachau mit den Innenstädten von Krems und Stein genießen. Die Gäste schätzen es, in der Fußgängerzone zu shoppen, einzukehren und die Weine zu verkosten. Sie besuchen die Kultureinrichtungen, die überregionale Akzente setzen, und werden Fans der ausverkauften Festivals. Sie bemerken, dass an den Wochentagen tausende Schüler und Studenten aus aller Welt die Stadt erobern. Übereinstimmend mit den Fachmedien stellen sie fest: Krems ist eine Kultur- und Universitätsstadt mit großem Potenzial. Kein Wunder, dass viele von ihnen davon schwärmen, hier wohnen und arbeiten oder studieren und forschen zu können.

Die Aufnahmen von Manuel Tauber-Romieri geben teils ungewöhnliche Einblicke aus Sicht eines Fotokünstlers in die Vielfalt der über 1000 Jahre alten Stadt. Er kam als suchender Gast und war bald begeistert von den zahlreichen Motiven und Eindrücken. Tausende Aufnahmen hat er mitgenommen, die nur zum Teil in diesen Bildband aufgenommen werden konnten.

Als Guide stand ihm mit Franz Schönfellner ein Kulturhistoriker zur Seite, der ein leidenschaftlicher Kremser ist. Er hat selbst bei den Recherchen immer wieder unbekannte Seiten von Krems entdecken dürfen. Nun begleitet er Sie mit den Textbeiträgen bei Ihrem Rundgang durch die Donaustadt. Beide stimmen nach ihren ausführlichen Recherchen überein, dass Krems an der Donau mit Recht international Beachtung findet und als Vorbild genommen wird. Sie sind sich einig, dass die mehrmals ausgezeichnete Musterstadt der Denkmalpflege auch für die kommenden Herausforderungen gut gerüstet ist. Als eine Stadt, die mit langer Erfahrung dynamisch

***Krems an der Donau** is one of Austria's most desirable cities to live in. A fact that is acknowledged time and time again. Not least by hundreds of thousands of tourists who savour the beauty of the Wachau region, a World Heritage Site, with the historic towns of Krems and Stein. Visitors love to shop in the pedestrian zone, stopping for refreshment and tasting the local wines. They visit the cultural venues, whose impact goes far beyond the region itself, and become fans of the sold-out festivals. They see how the city is taken over on weekdays by thousands of school pupils and students from all over the world. They agree with the specialist media who say that Krems is a culture and university city with great potential. It's no wonder that many of them would love to live and work, study and research here.*

Manuel Tauber-Romieri's photos, taken from the perspective of a photo artist, cast the diversity of the over 1,000-year-old city in a sometimes unexpected light. He came to the city as a questing visitor and was soon captivated by the wealth of subjects and impressions. He came away with thousands of photos, only a fraction of which could be included in this book.

To guide him he had Franz Schönfellner, a cultural historian who loves his native city with a passion. In the course of his research, Schönfellner also came across many aspects of Krems that he had not known about. Now his texts accompany you on your tour of the city on the Danube. Following their in-depth research, both men agree that Krems an der Donau rightly enjoys international recognition and is seen as an example to follow. They agree that the city, a winner of many awards as a model of historic and cultural preservation, is also well equipped for the coming challenges. As a city with long years of experience that allows it to stride confidently into a highly promising future.

REICHE VERGANGENHEIT
A RICH PAST

Die Statue der Fanny vom Galgenberg ist vor 36.000 Jahren hierhergekommen. Das Stadtwappen datiert aus 1305. Die reiche Geschichte prägt das Stadtbild von Krems.

The statue of Fanny *of Galgenberg arrived here 36,000 years ago. The city coat of arms dates from 1305. Wherever you look you find evidence of the city's rich history.*

links: Sgrafittohaus Margarethenstraße | *left: House with sgrafitto facade, Margarethenstraße*
ganz oben: Rathaus Krems | *top: Krems City Hall*
oben: Fanny vom Galgenberg/Museum Krems | *above: Fanny of Galgenberg/Krems Museum*

BASIS FÜR DIE ZUKUNFT
READY FOR THE FUTURE

Die Stadt ruht sich nicht auf den wohlerworbenen Lorbeeren aus. Krems ist schon seit Jahren nicht mehr das verträumte Städtchen an der Donau, sondern eine lebendige, urbane, ständig wachsende Donaumetropole. Die Zukunft ist gegenwärtig, sie manifestiert sich unverkennbar in den internationalen Bildungs- und Forschungseinrichtungen der boomenden Universitätsstadt.

In Krems an der Donau – dort wo andere Urlaub machen – leben, studieren und arbeiten zu dürfen, das wird ein Ziel für viele. Denn die Stadt entwickelt sich ständig weiter, sie wächst und rüstet sich für neue Herausforderungen. Als Kraftplatz der Bildung, als Wirtschafts- und Handelszentrum, als kultureller Mittelpunkt mit großen Kunsthäusern und ausverkauften Festivals, mit viel an Naturraum und Freizeitmöglichkeiten lässt Krems Lebensträume wahr

The city *does not live on past glories, however great these may be. The days are long gone when Krems was a small, sleepy town on the Danube. For years it has been a vibrant, urbane, constantly growing Danubian hub. The future is now. It is evident from the international education and research institutions in the thriving university town.*

Living, studying and working in Krems an der Donau, where others spend their holidays, has become the aim of many. Because the city is in constant flux, growing and preparing itself for new challenges. As an educational power point, a centre of trade and industry, a cultural hub with major art institutions and sold-out festivals, with extensive green spaces and leisure amenities Krems makes lifelong dreams come true.

Weingut Rabl

WEIN UND GENUSS
WINE AND HAUTE CUISINE

Im Weinland steht höchste Qualität für Genießer im Vordergrund. Das von der Kremser Agentur LWmedia veranstaltete wachau GOURMETfestival lädt alljährlich als Auftakt zur Verkostung der besten Weine.

In the wine region *the spotlight is on the very highest quality for epicureans. The wachau GOURMETfestival organized by the Krems agency LWmedia is the annual curtain-raiser to tastings of the best wines.*

Dominikanerkirche Krems | *Dominikanerkirche Krems*

1579

WOHLSTAND DURCH HANDEL
PROSPERITY THROUGH TRADE

Schon vor 1000 Jahren legten die Donauzillen in Krems-Stein an, um Wein zu exportieren. Der Donauhandel von damals prägt bis heute das eindrucksvolle Stadtbild.

Danube barges *were already landing in the Stein district of Krems to export wine 1,000 years ago. The river trade of those distant days still defines the city's arresting character.*

links: Steiner Landstraße 84 | *left: Steiner Landstraße 84*
oben: Blick auf Stein – Donaulände | *above: View of Stein – Donaulände*

Nächste Seite (von links oben im Uhrzeigersinn) | *next page (clockwise from top left)*
Schiffstation Stein | *Stein landing stage*
Rathaus Krems | *Krems City Hall*
Steiner Tor/Westfassade | *Steiner Tor/west facade*
Campus und Altstadt Stein | *Stein campus and old town*

Unesco-Weltkulturerbe, Musterstadt der Denkmalpflege, lebenswerteste Stadt Österreichs sind nur wenige der vielen Auszeichnungen für Krems. Die Donaustadt pflegt erfolgreich die Kultur des Wandels und hat sich dadurch in eine neue Städteliga katapultiert. Kunst und Bildung, dynamische Unternehmen, attraktive Gastronomie und Weinszene sowie zahlreiche weitere Bausteine machen Krems zu einer Vorzeigestadt.

UNESCO World Heritage Site, *model of historic preservation and the best Austrian city to live in: these are just some of the accolades bestowed on Krems. The city on the Danube successfully cultivates the culture of change, and this has catapulted it into a new league. Art and education, dynamic businesses, attractive restaurants and its wine join numerous other elements to make Krems a model city.*

Bis vor wenigen Jahrzehnten war die Donaustadt für die Gäste vor allem ein beliebtes Fotomotiv. Und natürlich als Weinstadt bekannt. Die erfolgreiche Geschichte prägt die Hausfassaden und vor allem die Bewohner, die vor 1000 Jahren von der speziellen Lage am Donaustrom am Ausgang der Wachau profitierten. Und sie stellen sich den aktuellen Herausforderungen. Heute ist Krems ein Musterbeispiel für gelungene Revitalisierung. Junges Leben strömt durch die Innenstadt, durch die international beachteten Kulturangebote und die Hochschulen und Universitäten.

Until a few decades ago, the city served visitors principally as a popular subject for photography. And of course it was known as a city of wine. Its successful history has left its mark on the facades of the buildings and especially on the inhabitants who, 1,000 years ago, profited from the town's favourable location on the Danube at the edge of the Wachau region. And today's citizens are meeting today's challenges. Modern Krems is a superb example of successful revitalisation. The city centre teems with young life, drawn by the internationally acclaimed cultural activities, the colleges and universities.

KLIMESCH SCHUHE
manera
ruefa

SALAMANDER

EINE ATTRAKTIVE MISCHUNG
AN ATTRACTIVE COMBINATION

Krems liegt an der Donau, auch wenn es der heutige Verlauf des Stromes nicht überall im Stadtbild vermuten lässt. Die Geschichte der Stromlandschaft ist zugleich eine Geschichte ihrer Umgestaltung und Veränderung. Als der zweitgrößte Fluss Europas ist die Donau eine wichtige Handelsverbindung zwischen Mittel- und Osteuropa. Sie war und ist ein opulenter Fischgrund und begünstigt Landwirtschaft und Tourismus. Der Stromabschnitt der Wachau ist ein kleiner, aber ganz besonderer Teil davon. Ein uralter Siedlungsraum, der von den Bewohnern über Jahrhunderte meist behutsam mitgeformt und verändert wurde. Die gekonnte Mischung aus Naturlandschaft und Siedlungsgebiet macht seine Attraktivität aus.

Die Donaustadt ist eingebettet in die steil ansteigenden Weinhänge, die die Landschaft prägen. Vor über 1200 Jahren setzte ein regelrechter Wettlauf um die Weinbauflächen in der Region ein. Denn sie garantierten gute Geschäftsgrundlagen für die Investitionen von Kirche und Staat, ebenso wie für Händler und Handwerker. So entstand mit Krems-Stein eine mittelalterliche Doppelstadt, die bald begehrter Siedlungsraum wurde. Die rasch steigende Finanzkraft der Kremserinnen und Kremser spiegelt sich in den kulturellen Leistungen wider. Die intensive Bautätigkeit aus der Gründungszeit formt bis heute die beiden Innenstädte von Krems und von Stein, die dank behutsamer Revitalisierung nicht nur beeindruckende Fotomotive, sondern vor allem eine hohe Lebensqualität bieten.

Unweit davon, wo früher die ersten Nomaden ihre Spuren und mittlerweile wertvollen Artefakte hinterließen, studieren heute die Studentinnen und Studenten der Donau-Universität Krems. Und östlich der Altstadtkerne findet sich ausreichend Platz für Industrie- und Wirtschaftsbetriebe. Nördlich und südlich davon bietet Krems in den Katastralgemeinden genügend Raum für neues Wohnen. Trotz so manch finsterer Zeiten im Laufe der Jahrhunderte konnte Krems seine Potenziale immer ausschöpfen und sich zu einer der beliebtesten Städte Österreichs entwickeln.

***Krems is on the Danube,** even though the course the river takes today means this is not apparent everywhere in the city. The story of the river landscape is also a story of its redevelopment and change. The second-longest river in Europe, the Danube is an important trade route between central and eastern Europe. It was, and still is, a fertile breeding ground for fish, and supports agriculture and tourism. The stretch through the Wachau may be short, but it has a very special character. An ancient settlement site that has been shaped and changed for centuries, usually prudently, by those who live there. Its attractiveness stems from the judicious interplay of countryside and human settlement.*

Krems nestles amid the steeply climbing vineyards that dominate the landscape. 1,200 years ago there was a veritable rush to grab the region's best wine-growing sites. This was because they guaranteed a sound basis for investments made by the church and state as well as for traders and craftsmen. The result was Krems and Stein, a medieval twin town that was soon to become a popular place to settle. The rapidly growing prosperity of the townsfolk is reflected in their cultural accomplishments. The intensive building that went on in the days of the city's foundation still forms the centres of both Krems and Stein to this day. Thanks to careful revitalisation, these two old towns now offer not just stunning subjects for photography, but also a high quality of life.

Nearby, where once the first nomads left their traces and several valuable artefacts, students in the Danube city of Krems now pursue their studies. And to the east of the old town centres there is plenty of room for industry and commerce. To the north and south, Krems has sufficient space for new housing in the cadastral municipalities. Despite several dark periods in the course of the centuries, Krems has always been able to fulfil its potential and is now one of Austria's most popular towns.

Vorige Seite: Täglicher Markt | *previous page: Täglicher Markt*

Mauterner Brücke | *Mautern Bridge*

GESEGNETE LANDSCHAFT
A BLESSED REGION

Die Donau ist internationaler Verkehrsweg, sie bringt die Touristenströme und schuf die Lage und das besondere Klima für den Weinbau in der Wachau.

***The Danube** is an international transport route, bringing crowds of tourists and creating the topography and unique climate for growing wine in the Wachau.*

Blick über Krems nach Göttweig | *View across Krems to Göttweig*

Nächste Seite: Am Ausgang der Wachau | *next page: The gateway to the Wachau*

MYTHOS WACHAU
WACHAU, THE MYTH

Die Wachau gilt als eines der schönsten Flusstäler Europas. Es sind zwar nur 33 Stromkilometer von Melk bis Krems, doch die haben es in sich.

The Wachau *is regarded as one of Europe's most beautiful river valleys. From Melk to Krems is only 33 km, but what a stretch it is!*

LEBEN AN DER DONAU
LIFE ON THE DANUBE

Die majestätisch dahingleitenden Donauschiffe bewegen große Handelsströme auf der Donau. Gerade in der Wachau begrüßen und verabschieden sie in der Saison tagtäglich tausende Touristen, die das Weltkulturerbe vom Wasser aus erleben wollen. Sie bringen den Unternehmen in der Region gute Umsätze und gehören zum Stadtbild von Krems-Stein.

Die Donau selbst wirkt dabei vertraut und ruhig. Dass das Leben mit dem Fluss ebenso Gefahren birgt, zeigt sich bei den großen Hochwasserkatastrophen. Bis ins 19. Jahrhundert wurden Krems und Stein regelmäßig überflutet, später wurde Krems mit einem Dammbau geschützt. Stein wurde weiterhin von Fluten heimgesucht. Es ist erst 20 Jahre her, dass die mobile Schutzanlage diesen Stadtteil schützt. Wobei dies natürlich nur bei statistisch berechneten hundertjährigen Hochwässern gilt und sich die Bewohner nach den jüngsten Erfahrungen, die nur knapp gut ausgingen, bewusst sind, dass irgendwann ein größeres kommen wird.

***The majestically** gliding Danube ships move large trade flows on the Danube. It is in the Wachau that they welcome and part from thousands of tourists every day who wish to experience the World Heritage Site from the water. They bring the region's businesses good turnovers and are part of the scenery of Krems-Stein.*

In the midst of all this, the Danube itself appears familiar and serene. That life on the river also poses a threat is shown by the major flood disasters. Until the 19th century, Krems and Stein were regularly flooded. Later, a dam was built to protect Krems. Stein continued to be prone to flooding. The mobile flood barrier that protects this district was installed only 20 years ago. Of course, this applies to the floods that, statistically, occur once every hundred years, and the population, having experienced recent floods that only just fell short of a major disaster, knows that one will come sooner or later.

oben: Donauradweg bei der Schiffstation | *above: Danube cycle path by the landing stage*
rechts: Donau nach Osten mit Bahnbrücke | *right: The Danube looking east with railway bridge*

DE 16259

WIRTSCHAFTS-STROM
BUSINESS RIVER

In Krems-Stein kreuzte sich einst ein Handelsweg von Venedig nach Nordeuropa mit dem Donauhandelsweg. Ersterer fiel weg, die Schifffahrt blieb ein Motor für die Region.

Once upon a time, *a trade route from Venice to northern Europe intersected with the Danube trade route in Krems-Stein. The first was abandoned, while shipping remained a driving force in the region.*

Stadtteil Stein von der Brücke aus | *Stein from the bridge*

DIE DOPPELSTADT
THE TWIN TOWN

Eines der ungelösten Rätsel der Stadtgeschichte ist, warum in unmittelbarer Nähe zunächst zwei Siedlungen entstanden, die Vorläuferinnen des heutigen namensgebenden Krems und der nunmehrigen Katastralgemeinde Stein. Sie wurden jedenfalls bald aus finanztechnischen Gründen zur landesherrlichen Doppelstadt Krems-Stein vereint, trotzdem mit für lange Zeit getrennten Stadtmauern und eigener Infrastruktur. Vermutlich ist dies auf die uralten Handelswege und die beiden strategischen Siedlungen aus der Slawenzeit zurückzuführen, eine auf dem Höhenrücken gegenüber dem heutigen Mautern und die zweite östlich davon am Weg über das Kremstal nach Norden.

Dazwischen lag bis ins 19. Jahrhundert eine Sumpf- und Aulandschaft, die erst durch die Donauregulierungen dauerhaft bewohnbar wurde. Heute sind Krems und Stein längst zusammengewachsen. Das eigentliche Stadtzentrum ist nunmehr in Krems, der Stadtteil Stein entwickelt sich zum Kultur- und Bildungszentrum der Region.

One of the unsolved mysteries *of the city's history is why two settlements arose in such close proximity, the forerunners of today's eponymous municipality of Krems and the cadastral municipality of Stein. What is certain is that for financial reasons they were soon united as the sovereign twin town of Krems-Stein, although they retained their own city walls and infrastructure for a long time. This was presumably because of the ancient trade routes and the two strategic settlements from the time of the Slavs, one on the ridge opposite modern Mautern and the other to the east of it heading north across the Krems valley.*

Until the 19th century, swamp and water meadows lay between them. This area did not become permanently habitable until river regulation measures were taken on the Danube. Today, Krems and Stein have long been contiguous. The town centre proper is now in Krems, while Stein is emerging as the region's culture and education centre.

SALAMANDER
MOHR
krems
FLOH MARKT
AM SAMSTAG
DEN 01.10.16

PASS
BILDER
AKTION
9,90
9,90

VOM LEBEN IM ZENTRUM
ON LIFE IN THE CENTRE

Elf Katastralgemeinden zählt Krems nördlich und südlich der Donau, die jüngsten kamen erst 1972 dazu. Ihr Mittelpunkt ist die Innenstadt von Krems. Im Mittelalter mussten die Siedler hier zwangsläufig zusammenrücken, ließ ihnen der einstmals ungezähmte wilde Fluss kaum Platz für ihre Häuser und Werkstätten. Selbst die Stadtmauern konnten sie Jahrhunderte hindurch nicht vor den Fluten der Donau schützen. Doch die Kremser konnten damit umgehen und die Stadt entwickelte sich prächtig.

Hinter dem Steiner Tor, dem einzigen der vier Stadttore von Krems, das das 19. Jahrhundert überdauerte, öffnet sich heute die hoch frequentierte Fußgängerzone. Sie teilt sich auf der Höhe des Kremser Rathauses in die Obere und die Untere Landstraße. Das Rathaus als weltliches Verwaltungszentrum wird von zwei sorgsam restaurierten Kirchenjuwelen flankiert, der gotischen Bürgerspitalkirche und der barocken Pfarrkirche, die sich stolz „Dom der Wachau" nennt. Die beiden Plätze beim Rathaus, der Pfarrplatz und der Tägliche Markt, waren so wie alle größeren freien Flächen seit dem Mittelalter Zentren der Nahversorger und der fahrenden Händler. Am Täglichen Markt stand zudem früher ein öffentlicher Brunnen, der schon vor 500 Jahren mit Quellwasser vom Berg her gespeist wurde.

Hoch über dem Pfarrplatz und der Stadtpfarrkirche thront die Piaristenkirche, die ihr heutiges Aussehen zeitgleich mit dem Wiener Stephansdom erhielt. Mit Recht darf sie sich als dessen „kleine Schwester" bezeichnen, waren doch damals die gleichen Bauleute wie in Wien am Werk. Unweit vom Piaristenkloster kündet die sogenannte Gozzoburg vom Reichtum eines landesfürstlichen Verwaltungsbeamten. Er ließ wahrscheinlich aus eigener Tasche ein wahrhaft fürstliches Gebäude errichten, das im Mittelalter weit über die Landesgrenzen hinaus bekannt war. Heute ist Krems eine Musterstadt für gelungene Revitalisierung, in der mit Verstand und Geschick in die meist jahrhundertealten Häuser investiert wird.

Krems has eleven cadastral communities *to the north and south of the Danube. The most recent were incorporated in 1972. Their centre is Krems Old Town. In the Middle Ages the settlers had no choice but to huddle together since the river, wild and untamed in those days, offered scant room for houses and workshops. For centuries, not even the city walls were able to protect them from the flood waters of the Danube. But the people of Krems coped, and the town thrived.*

Behind the Steiner Tor, the only city gate in Krems that survived beyond the 19th century, the bustling pedestrian zone now unfolds. By the City Hall it splits into Obere Landstraße and Untere Landstraße. The City Hall, the seat of secular administration, is flanked by two carefully restored gems of churches: the Gothic Bürgerspitalkirche and the Baroque parish church that proudly calls itself "the cathedral of the Wachau". Like all large open spaces, the two squares by the City Hall, Pfarrplatz and Täglicher Markt, were centres for local provisions and itinerant merchants from the Middle Ages onward. A public well also once stood on Tägliche Markt whose water came from the hills as early as 500 years ago.

High above Pfarrplatz and the Stadtpfarrkirche sits the Piaristenkirche, which was given its modern appearance at the same time as St. Stephen's in Vienna. The Piarist church can justly claim to be the latter's "little sister" since it was built by the same people as Vienna's cathedral. Not far from the Piarist monastery, the so-called Gozzoburg provides evidence of the wealth of an official to the local ruler. The official had a truly magnificent house built, probably at his own expense, whose fame spread far and wide in the Middle Ages. Today, Krems is a model of successful revitalisation in the course of which money is spent judiciously on buildings that are for the most part centuries old.

Kirchengasse/Bürgerspitalkirche | *Kirchengasse/Bürgerspitalkirche*

MITTEL PUR

THE SO THE MI AGES

Im sogenannten Säng Schornstein soll schon genächtigt haben, der chige Lyriker des Mitte

In the so-called Sänge *ney, Walther von der V dieval German-speakin spent the night.*

Sängerho

GESCHICHTE HAUTNAH
HISTORY YOU CAN TOUCH

Enge Gassen führen in der Altstadt weg von der Landstraße zu den Kirchen und hinauf zur Gozzoburg. Die pittoresken Fotomotive sind Zeitzeugen einer lebhaften Vergangenheit.

In the historic centre, *narrow lanes lead away from Landstraße to the churches and up to the Gozzoburg. The picturesque photo subjects bear witness to a lively past.*

ganz oben: Gasse in Stein | *top: Street in Stein*
oben: Wehrmauer beim Pulverturm | *above: Defensive wall by the magazine*
rechts: Zubau zur Gozzoburg | *right: Annex to the Gozzoburg*

1706

FÜR GOTTES SEGEN FOR GOD'S BLESSINGS

Die Piaristenkirche wurde von den anerkanntesten Bauleuten parallel zum Stephansdom zu Wien geschaffen und ist ein sehenswertes Baujuwel der Gotik.

The Piaristenkirche *was built at the same time as St. Stephen's Cathedral in Vienna by the most celebrated builders of the age. It is a magnificent Gothic jewel.*

BILDUNG IM FOKUS
SPOTLIGHT ON EDUCATION

Aus dem mittelalterlichen Handelsplatz Stein wurde in den letzten Jahrzehnten eine boomende Kultur- und Universitätsstadt mit Blick nach vorne.

In recent decades, *the medieval trading post of Stein has become a thriving culture and university town with its gaze fixed firmly forward.*

STEIN: GENIALE GENE
STEIN: IT'S IN THE GENES

Den Steinern liegen Kunst und Forschung in den Genen. Ludwig Ritter von Köchel wurde als Sammler und Forscher durch das Köchel-Verzeichnis, eine penible Zusammenstellung der Werke von Wolfgang Amadeus Mozart, weltberühmt. Er wurde in Stein geboren, ebenso wie Rosina Altmann, eine der Großmütter des Salzburger Musikgenies. Dazu ist Stein mit gutem Grund stolz auf Martin Johann Schmidt, der als begnadeter Barockmaler den Ruf der Stadt als „Kremser Schmidt" weit über die Landesgrenzen hinaustrug. Dass der Name der Doppelstadt Krems-Stein dabei auf Krems reduziert wurde, stört die Steiner bis heute ein wenig. Dafür wird die Justizanstalt gerne dem Stadtteil Stein namentlich zugeordnet, was bald Geschichte sein dürfte. Doch genug der lokalen Unpässlichkeiten. Stein war schon lange eine Stadt der Künstler und der Forscher und sie hat sich nicht auf den Lorbeeren ausgeruht, sondern geradezu hinaufkatapultiert in eine neue Epoche.

Früher dominierten die Lesehöfe auswärtiger Klöster und Stifte das Stadtbild von Stein. Über 50 Klöster hatten in der Region ihre Wirtschaftsanlagen. Sie verwalteten ihre Weingärten, schenkten den Wein – oft sehr zum Ärger der Bürger – vor Ort aus und ließen vor allem den hier gekelterten Wein in Fässern durch die Landstraße zu den Schiffen rollen. Und sie stellten so die Arbeitsplätze für die meisten Inwohner des Stadtteiles.

Kein Schiff kam ohne Gegenfuhre, somit wurde der Donauhandel das wirtschaftliche Rückgrat der rasanten Entwicklung von Stein. Obwohl Josef II. so manche Klöster aufheben ließ und ihnen die Besitzungen entzog, sind die großen Wirtschaftshöfe nach wie vor in Stein präsent. Und die Personenschifffahrt erlebt eine Hochblüte – nicht nur wenn die Marille im Frühjahr die Wachau in ein Blütenmeer verwandelt.

Heute sind es die pulsierenden Kultureinrichtungen und die Universitäten, die Stein prägen. Hunderttausende Touristen und jährlich fast 15.000 Studentinnen und Studenten erfüllen den Stadtteil Stein mit jungem Leben.

Art and research *are in the genes of the people of Stein. Ludwig Ritter von Köchel achieved worldwide fame as a collector and scientist thanks to the Köchel Catalogue, a meticulously compiled register of the works of Wolfgang Andreas Mozart. He was born in Stein, as was Rosina Altmann, a grandmother of the musical genius from Salzburg. Stein is also justly proud of Martin Johann Schmidt, a gifted Baroque painter whose sobriquet "Kremser Schmidt" made the town's name known far beyond the borders of Austria. The truncation of the twin town's name of Krems-Stein to Krems still rankles with the people of Stein a little, even today. On the other hand, the prison is widely associated with the name of Stein, though this may soon be consigned to the history books. But enough of these local grievances. Stein had long been a town of artists and scientists, and far from resting on its laurels it has fairly catapulted itself into a new era.*

In the past, Stein was dominated by the vineyards of foreign monasteries and abbeys. Over 50 monasteries had their farming operations in the region. They managed their vineyards, served their wine in the town itself – very often to the annoyance of the locals – and had the wine they pressed here rolled down Landstraße in barrels to the ships. Consequently, they were the biggest employers in the district.

No ship arrived unladen, which made trade on the Danube the economic backbone of Stein's rapid development. Although Josef II dissolved many monasteries and seized their property, the large farms remain in Stein. Passenger transport on the river is experiencing a golden age – and not just when the apricot trees turn the Wachau into a sea of blossom in spring.

Today, it is the vibrant culture institutions and universities that give Stein its character. Hundreds of thousands of tourists and nearly 15,000 students every year fill Stein with young life.

TOR ZUM WEINLAND
GATEWAY TO WINE COUNTRY

Das sogenannte Rebentor über der Steiner Altstadt ist eines der wenigen erhaltenen Stadttore. Der Name erinnert daran, dass unmittelbar dahinter die Weingärten liegen.

The so-called Rebentor *above Stein old town is one of the few surviving city gates. The name ("Vine Gate") is a reminder that vineyards lie just behind it.*

Am Rebentor | *By the Rebentor*

Nächste Seite (von links oben im Uhrzeigersinn)
next page (clockwise from top left)
Karikaturmuseum | *Karikaturmuseum*
Obere Landstraße | *Obere Landstraße*
Dom der Wachau | *Wachau Cathedral*
Dachlandschaft über Stein | *Roofs over Stein*

Die Geschichte der Donaustadt führt 36.000 Jahre zurück. Zu den ersten Siedlern, zu Kriegen und Katastrophen, aber auch zur Fertigstellung des Hochwasserschutzes Stein im Jahr 1995. Im gleichen Jahr wurden die Kunsthalle und der Campus Krems eröffnet – viel beachtete Beispiele für die stete Weiterentwicklung von Krems.

***The history** of the city on the Danube goes back 36,000 years. To the first settlers, to wars and disasters, but also to the completion of Stein's flood control installation in 1995. That same year, the Kunsthalle and Campus Krems – highly regarded examples of the constant evolution of Krems – were opened.*

Charakteristisch für die rasante Entwicklung der Stadt ist die Bautätigkeit am Campus Krems. Innerhalb weniger Jahre entstand am Fuße der Weinberge ein Hochschulgelände, das ideale Voraussetzungen für Ausbildung und Forschung mit Partnern auf der ganzen Welt schafft. Und die Zahl der Forschungseinrichtungen rund um die Donau-Universität Krems, die IMC Fachhochschule Krems und die Karl Landsteiner Privatuniversität steigt ständig. Auch unweit des Campus Krems bezeugt eine rege Bautätigkeit für Studenten aus aller Welt das rasant wachsende Bildungsangebot. All You Need is Krems, so bringt es die IMC Fachhochschule auf den Punkt.

The construction work carried out at Campus Krems is typical of the city's rapid development. In the space of only a few years, a university campus was created at the foot of the vineyards, offering perfect conditions for education and research with partners all over the world. And the number of research institutions around the Danube University Krems, the IMC University of Applied Sciences Krems and the Karl Landsteiner Private University continues to increase. Intensive building work not far from Campus Krems also testifies to the growing educational opportunities for students from all over the world. As the IMC University of Applied Sciences so succinctly puts it: All You Need is Krems.

ALUMNI
FH KREMS
SPONSION
IMC Graduation

imc ALUMNI FH KREMS
SPONSION
Graduation

Word Online
Fundamentals of Law: Private and Public Law
The Austrian Judicial System
State and government of Austria

WO KARRIEREN STARTEN
WHERE CAREERS START

Schon vor 500 Jahren studierten Bürgersöhne aus Krems an den bedeutendsten deutschsprachigen Universitäten Europas. Und doch glaubten bis vor wenigen Jahrzehnten nur wenige daran, dass aus Krems in kürzester Zeit eine Universitätsstadt mit Bildungseinrichtungen auf höchstem Niveau würde. Die erste weiterführende Bildungseinrichtung in Krems war die sogenannte Lehrerbildungsanstalt, aus der sich die Kirchlich Pädagogische Hochschule entwickelte.

Die IMC Fachhochschule Krems erweckte das barocke Piaristenkloster und die stattliche Gozzoburg im Zentrum von Krems zu neuem Leben. Hier und auf dem Campusgelände in Stein bietet sie ein auf Wirtschaft, Gesundheit und Life Sciences ausgerichtetes Studienangebot mit internationaler Ausrichtung. Sie kann mit Stolz auf unzählige Erfolge bei nationalen und internationalen Rankings verweisen.

Der Campus entstand rund um eine ehemalige Tabakfabrik in Stein, die heute Teil der Donau-Universität Krems ist. Als einzige Universität für Weiterbildung im deutschsprachigen Raum hat sie aktuell 9000 Studierende aus mehr als 90 Ländern. Die intensive Forschungsarbeit in Kooperation mit internationalen Partnern ist eine ausgezeichnete Basis für eine praxisbezogene Ausbildung. Und die Karl Landsteiner Privatuniversität punktet mit höchster Kompetenz in Gesundheitswissenschaften und Medizin.

Und vor dem Linzer Tor in Stein wächst in rasantem Tempo die Danube Private University, die ein staatlich akkreditiertes Studium der Zahnmedizin bietet. Jährlich steigende Studentenzahlen belegen den Erfolg aller Institutionen. 2017 zählen die Statistiken über 25.000 Schülerinnen und Schüler, die täglich in Krems lernen, studieren und forschen. Krems braucht damit keinen Vergleich scheuen, es hat sich zum Bildungszentrum entwickelt, das Studierende, Vortragende und Partner aus allen Kontinenten begrüßt.

As early as 500 years ago *sons from middle-class families in Krems studied at the foremost German-speaking universities in Europe. Despite this, until a few decades ago few people believed that Krems could become a university town with educational institutions of the highest standard so quickly. The first tertiary education institution in Krems was the teacher training institute from which the University College for Teacher Education of Christian Churches emerged.*

The IMC University of Applied Sciences Krems gave the Baroque Piarist monastery and the imposing Gozzoburg in the centre of Krems a new lease of life. Here and on the campus in Stein it offers courses focusing on business, health and life sciences with an international orientation. It can point proudly to countless successes in national and international listings.

The campus was built around a disused tobacco factory in Stein which today is part of the Danube University Krems. The only university of continuing education in the German-speaking world, it currently has 9,000 students from more than 90 countries. The intensive research conducted in cooperation with international partners is an excellent basis for practice-oriented training. And the Karl Landsteiner Private University distinguishes itself with superlative competence in health sciences and medicine.

And in front of the Linzer Tor in Stein, the Danube Private University is appearing at incredible speed and will offer state-approved degree courses in dentistry. Student numbers that increase every year underline the success of all the institutions. The figures for 2017 show that over 25,000 school pupils and students learn, study and conduct research in Krems every day. So Krems need not fear any comparisons; it has evolved into a centre of education that welcomes students, lecturers and partners from every continent.

Vorige Seite: IMC Fachhochschule am Campus | *previous page: IMC University of Applied Sciences on the Campus*

Lehrsaal im Piaristenkloster | *Lecture theatre in the Piarist monastery*

RÄUME ZUM DENKEN
ROOMS FOR THOUGHT

Für modernste Ansprüche wurden historische Räume an der Donau-Universität Krems zur idealen Atmosphäre für ein Studium mit internationaler Ausrichtung adaptiert.

Historic rooms *at the Danube University Krems were adapted to today's requirements to create the ideal atmosphere for study with an international orientation.*

Haupteingang Donau-Universität
Danube University main entrance

AP 30.000
Rundfunk
Broadcast
AP 27040 W426
AP 27080 L7441
AP 27080 N946-33
AP 27240 E312(2)-54
AP 27420 L442
AP 27420 R834(2)-66
AP 27500 P238
AP 27500 R718-2671
AP 27760 F654
AP 27760 F654(6)
AP 27760 P4581(3)
AP 27760 S459
AP 28400 B888
AP 28440 S781-22
AP 28440 H8771
AP 29000 F897-21+1
AP 29000 F897-21+2
AP 29000 S979(2)
AP 29200 S947-19
AP 29400 M4231
AP 29420 F449
AP 29420 M994
AP 31500 B937-11
AP 32200 D779
AP 32320 T787
AP 29700 V47
Television
DIE QUALITÄT AKADEMISCHER LEHRE
Christian Doelker Kulturtechnik Fernsehen
RUPERT MURDOCH
Claudia Fischer (Hg.): Hochschul-Radios
Sturm/Zirbik: Die Radio-Station
Norbert Bakenhus: Das Lokalradio
NDER UND DER MEDIENMARKT
PAUL
Bilder des Krieges
Krieg der Bilder
Die Fernsehreportage
Zehrt: Hörfunk-Nachrichten
Bilanz und Perspektiven
Viva MTV! reloaded
AP 33200 S643
AP 33700 H628-3
AP 33700 M563-2
AP 34000 D651
AP 34000 P926-4
AP 34000 Z67-489
AP 34050 H887-CD
AP 34050 H887-CD+2
AP 34050 T886
AP 34250 B625-5
AP 34250 F529-26
AP 34600 G455
AP 34620 S936
AP 34620 B167-24
AP 34620 S864-14
AP 35120 M489-2001
AP 35580 E69
AP 35620 K89-5
AP 36080 P324
AP 36080 W833-46
AP 36080 Z44-25
AP 36160 P334-32
AP 36280 Z73(2)-1
AP 36360 S3491+2

JETZT RAUCHEN DIE KÖPFE
FROM FACTORY TO FACULTY

Vor hundert Jahren rollten am heutigen Campus-Areal, eingebettet in die Weinlandschaft der Wachau, fast 800 Arbeiterinnen in mühsamer Handarbeit die Virginia-Zigarre. Sie war ein Exportschlager zu Zeiten der Donaumonarchie.

Heute beherbergt das ehemalige Kesselhaus der Tabakfabrik mit seinem markanten Schlot, wo der Dampf für die Maschinen, Filter- und Belüftungsanlagen erzeugt wurde, ein Programmkino und eine Filmbar. Und die Arbeitsräume und Trocknungslager der Fabrik – immer schon mit strengstem Rauchverbot wegen der Brandgefahr – wurden zu Denk- und Forschungswerkstätten für die Zukunft. Aus dem historischen Hauptgebäude wurde ein Teil der Donau-Universität. Neubauten in ausgezeichneter architektonischer Qualität für die Universität und für alle weiteren Partner vor Ort wurden angegliedert und beigefügt.

Am Campus Krems stehen nun modernste Lehr- und Forschungseinrichtungen für die beiden Universitäten und die IMC Fachhochschule zur Verfügung. Institutionen aus Wissenschaft und Kultur, wie das Ernst Krenek Institut und das Archiv der Zeitgenossen, haben die Bildungseinrichtungen am Hochschulgelände als geschätzte Partner in Lehre und Forschung.

A hundred years ago *nearly 800 women worked on the site of today's campus amid the scenic vineyards of the Wachau, painstakingly rolling Virginia cigars by hand. During the Habsburg monarchy, the cigars were exported in huge numbers.*

Today, the tobacco factory's former boiler house with its distinctive chimney, where steam for the machinery, filter and ventilation systems was generated, houses an arthouse cinema and a movie bar. And the factory's workrooms and drying stores, where smoking was always strictly prohibited owing to the fire hazard, have become think tanks and research workshops for the future. The historic main building became part of the Danube University. New buildings of outstanding architectural quality were affiliated and added for the university and all the other partners on the site.

At the Krems Campus, state-of-the-art teaching and research facilities are now available for the two universities and the IMC IMC University of Applied Sciences. Scientific and cultural institutions, such as the Ernst Krenek Institute and the Archives of Contemporary Arts, have the education institutions on the university campus as valued partners for teaching and research.

EINFACH INSPIRIEREND
SIMPLY INSPIRING

Studienservicecenter, Bibliothek, Kultur- und Sportangebote, komfortable Unterkünfte, ein Kindergarten und vieles mehr bieten die bestmögliche Umgebung für Lernen und Forschen.

A study service centre, *library, culture and sports facilities, comfortable accommodation, a kindergarten and much more provide the perfect environment for learning and research.*

ganz oben: am Campus | *top: On the Campus*
oben: Alte Tabakfabrik, heute Kindergarten | *above: Former tobacco factory, now a kindergarten*
rechts: Café Virginier | *right: Café Virginier*
Nächste Seite: Universitätsgebäude | *next page: University building*

14.00 montag bis freitag 8.00-18.00 samstag 8.00-14.00 montag bis frei
tag 8.00-18.00 samstag 8.00-14.00 montag bis freitag 8.00-18.00 samstag 8.00-
Coca-Cola
Warme Küche 11-14°°

PARTNER FÜR DIE GESUNDHEIT
PARTNER FOR HEALTHCARE

Die Karl Landsteiner Privatuniversität für Gesundheitswissenschaften forscht und lehrt in enger Kooperation mit Kliniken und Wirtschaftspartnern in richtungweisenden Feldern der Gesundheitswissenschaften und Medizin.

***The Karl Landsteiner Private University** of Health Sciences researches and teaches in pioneering fields of health sciences and medicine in close cooperation with clinics and business partners.*

RÄUME MIT PERSPEKTIVEN
ROOMS WITH GOOD PROSPECTS

Eingebettet in die Naturlandschaft und dennoch nahe beim Stadtzentrum liegt der Campus Krems. Die Infrastruktur stimmt, das Areal gehört den Radfahrern und Fußgängern und bietet vielfältige Räume zur Erholung.

Nestling *in the countryside, yet still close to the town centre, is Campus Krems. The amenities are ideal: the grounds belong to cyclists and pedestrians and offer many different ways of relaxing.*

Zeitgenössische Kunst am Campus
Contemporary art on the Campus

ANGEBOTE FÜR ALLE
SOMETHING FOR EVERYONE

Der Weinbau gehört in Krems einfach dazu. Fachschule, VinoHAK und Kolleg für Weinmanagement sind drei Säulen der Weinbauschule. Vom Traktorführerschein bis zum „International Wine Business", das Bildungsangebot ist reichhaltig.

***Viniculture** is quite simply part of Krems. The professional school, commercial school and the college of wine management are three pillars of training in viniculture. From learning to drive a tractor to the international wine business: a huge variety of courses is available.*

Designverbundglas – Kunstwerke
Atelier Illuminare

EXZELLENTE PERFORMANCE
EXCELLENT PERFORMANCE

In der Tourismusstadt Krems ist eine der führenden Tourismusschulen Österreichs beheimatet. Absolventen der HLF Krems trifft man mittlerweile in führenden Unternehmen auf der ganzen Welt.

***The tourist city of Krems** is home to one of Austria's leading tourism schools. Former pupils of HLF Krems can now be found working for leading companies the world over.*

links: Lehrrestaurant | *left: Teaching restaurant*
ganz oben: Lehrküche | *top: Teaching kitchen*
oben: HLF Krems, Tourismusschulen | *above: HLF Krems, tourism schools*

Nächste Seite (von links oben im Uhrzeigersinn) | *next page (clockwise from top left)*
International School | *International School*
Universitätsbibliothek | *University library*

Eine breite Palette an Aus- und Weiterbildungsangeboten, egal ob Englisch im Kindergarten oder mannigfaltige Kurse an der Volkshochschule bis zu den Hochschulen – Krems lebt die Bildung. Jüngstes Beispiel ist die zweisprachige International School, wo in Deutsch und in Englisch modernste pädagogische Konzepte realisiert werden.

A wide range *of training and further education courses, such as English at kindergarten or numerous courses at the community college or universities – Krems lives for education. The most recent example is the bilingual International School where the very latest educational concepts are put into practice in German and English.*

Die Kulturstadt Krems kann auf ein reiches Erbe und gemeinsam hochgehaltene Traditionen aufbauen. Die Kunstmeile Krems ist 20 Jahre jung und hat zahlreiche Magneten, die Gäste aus nah und fern anziehen. Und die Künstler treffen sich heute gerne in den etablierten Ausstellungshäusern und Galerien, auf international beachteten Festivals und zu vielen weiteren Events im Jahreskreislauf. Vom NÖ Literaturhaus bis zur Volkskultur bietet die Stadt ihren Bewohnern ein abwechslungsreiches Kulturangebot, um das sie viele beneiden.

As a city of culture, Krems can build on a rich heritage and traditions preserved by joint efforts. The Krems Art Mile is 20 years young and has numerous attractions that draw visitors from near and far. And today the artists enjoy meeting at the established exhibition venues and galleries, at internationally recognised festivals and at many other events during the course of a year. From the Lower Austrian Literaturhaus to folk culture, the city offers a wide variety of cultural activities to its inhabitants who are the envy of many as a result.

KARIKATUR
HADERER
4 RÄDERN
Comic und
tur
R DEIX!

REICH AN KUNST
A WEALTH OF ART

Schon lange kommen Gäste, die das reiche kulturelle Erbe zu schätzen wissen, immer wieder zurück nach Krems. Publikumsmagneten waren zunächst die opulent ausgestatteten Kirchen und die ersten großen Kunstausstellungen mit Leihgaben aus Museen. Heute ist die Kunstmeile mit nostalgiefreien Zonen dazugekommen, mit großen Themen- und Einzelausstellungen arrivierter und aktueller Kunst, die europaweit wahrgenommen werden. In der Landesgalerie haben Kunsthalle, Karikaturmuseum und Forum Frohner ab 2018 eine attraktive Partnerin, die weitere Besucherströme bringt.

Kunstmeile, Museen, Galerien, Kunst im öffentlichen Raum, beispielgebende Architektur, Konzerte, Programmkino und viele weitere Kunst- und Kulturangebote machen die Fülle der Kulturstadt Krems aus. Im Rahmen der Festivals kommen zeitgenössische Künstlerinnen und Künstler aus der ganzen Welt nach Krems und bringen der einst verträumten Wachaustadt völlig neue Impulse. Die Leiterinnen und Leiter der verschiedenen Einrichtungen haben sich der hohen Qualität verpflichtet und das Ergebnis gibt ihnen recht. Trotz der scheinbar geringen Größe der Wachaumetropole haben sich hier Kultureinrichtungen in einer Dichte wie selten an einem Ort zusammengefunden. Kein Wunder, dass Krems immer wieder den Titel der „heimlichen Kulturhauptstadt des Landes Niederösterreich“ für sich beansprucht, wenngleich die Konkurrenten hochaktiv sind.

Eine Vielzahl von Verkaufsgalerien und Kunsthändlern sucht die Nähe dieser Einrichtungen. Und auch die heimischen Kunstschaffenden bleiben nicht auf der Strecke. Konsequenterweise verzeichnet die Musikschule jährlich unzählige Nachwuchspreise für ihre Talente. Dazu laden junge Kunstschaffende in kleine Galerien und zu Konzerten. Ein Audioguide der Ludwig-Ritter-von Köchel-Gesellschaft ermög-

For years, *visitors who appreciate the rich cultural heritage have returned to Krems time and time again. The crowds first came to see the superbly furnished churches and the first major art exhibitions featuring loans from museums. Today, the Art Mile has been added with its nostalgia-free zones and major themed and solo exhibitions presenting established and modern art that attract attention all over Europe. From 2018, the Landesgalerie joins the Kunsthalle, Karikaturmuseum and Forum Frohner as an attractive partner that will draw even more crowds.*

The Art Mile, museums, galleries, art in public places, pioneering architecture, concerts, arthouse cinema and many other art and culture activities constitute the wealth of Krems, the culture city. Contemporary artists from all over the world come to Krems for the festivals, bringing entirely fresh ideas to the once sleepy town in the Wachau. Those in charge of the various institutions have committed themselves to high quality, and the results show that they are right to do so. Despite its apparent small size, the city has attracted culture institutions in numbers rarely found in comparable towns. No wonder, then, that Krems repeatedly lays claim to the title of "Secret culture capital of the province of Lower Austria", even if its rivals are very active.

Many galleries that sell art and other art dealers seek to be near these institutions. And local artists are not ignored either. It is therefore only logical that the music school pupils win countless young musicians' awards every year. In addition, young artists showcase their talents at small galleries and concerts. With an audio guide from the Ludwig Ritter von Köchel Society, visitors can also take a historical and musical stroll, following in the footsteps of Mozart and Beethoven. Krems is constantly producing something new and proves that culture is lived as a community.

QUALITÄT VERPFLICHTET
QUALITY MEANS COMMITMENT

Die Mischung auf der Kunstmeile stimmt: große Ausstellungen, zeitgenössische Arbeiten internationaler Künstler, Kunst zum Ausleihen, Artists in residence, Musik und Literatur.

The blend *on the Art Mile is just right: major exhibitions, contemporary works by international artists, art to borrow, artists in residence, music and literature.*

FORUM FÜR DIALOG
FORUM FOR DIALOGUE

Arbeiten von Adolf Frohner und aktuelle Themen der Gegenwartskunst, kulturelle und gesellschaftliche Veranstaltungen machen den Minoritenplatz zum Treffpunkt der Kulturszene.

Works by Adolf Frohner *and current subjects of contemporary art, plus cultural and social events make Minoritenplatz a place where the culture scene meets.*

MINORITENPLATZ

GOTIK TRIFFT GEGENWART
GOTHIC MEETS CONTEMPORARY

Die Kunstmeile ist tatsächlich eine Meile. Die gotische Dominikanerkirche und das barocke Kloster in der Innenstadt von Krems laden zu zeitgenössischen Kunsterlebnissen und ins Stadtmuseum mit dem Kremser Senf.

The Art Mile *really is a mile. The Gothic Dominikanerkirche and the Baroque monastery in Krems city centre invite visitors to experience contemporary art as well as the City Museum with Krems mustard.*

ganz oben: Karikaturmuseum Krems | *top: Karikaturmuseum Krems*
oben: Artothek NÖ | *above: Lower Austrian Artothek*
rechts: Moderne Galerie im Museum Krems | *right: Moderne Galerie in Krems Museum*

KUNST FINDET RAUM
ART FINDS ROOM

Kunstgenuss in historischen Räumen, das ist eine bewährte Mischung, die seit Jahrzehnten das besondere Flair der Kulturstadt ausmacht.

Appreciating art *in historic rooms is a combination that has proved its value for decades and constitutes the culture city's unique flair.*

kärnten hoch drei

EINFACH ZUM MITNEHMEN
ART TO GO

Bunt und abwechslungsreich ist das Kulturleben in Krems. Und manchmal bleibt man an einem der zahlreichen Exponate hängen und möchte es gerne mit nach Hause nehmen. Nicht als bloße Erinnerung, sondern einfach, weil es gefällt und man den geeigneten Platz daheim schon vor Augen hat. Und auch dafür findet sich in Krems eine Lösung.

Zahlreiche Galerien bieten Kunstwerke zum Verkauf. Wie die Galerie Kopriva am Dominikanerplatz im Stadtzentrum, wo Kunstfreunde Bilder und Skulpturen erwerben können. Rund um die Kunstmeile laden neben etablierten Einrichtungen wie die Galerie Stadtpark oder die Galerie Göttlicher in Stein viele junge Initiativen zum Kunstgenuss.

Oder sie probieren Kunst to go und lassen sich dabei von einem unabhängigen Expertenteam beraten. Die Bilder- und Grafiksammlung des Landes Niederösterreich steht in der Artothek an der Kunstmeile offen. Die leihen das gewählte Exponat aus, garantiert unbürokratisch und einfach.

Cultural life *in Krems is colourful and varied. And sometimes one of the many exhibits reaches out and grabs you, making you want to take it home with you. Not just as a souvenir, but simply because you like it and have already thought of the perfect place to put it at home. Krems has the answer to that, too.*

Many galleries have art for sale. One is Galerie Kopriva on Dominikanerplatz in the city centre. Here, art aficionados can buy pictures and sculptures. Around the Art Mile, many new initiatives have joined well-established institutions such as Galerie Stadtpark and Galerie Göttlicher in Stein in inviting visitors to enjoy art.

Or they try art to go and take advice from an independent team of experts. The collection of pictures and graphic works of the province of Lower Austria can be viewed in the Artothek on the Art Mile. Selected works are available for lending – no fuss and no bureaucracy, that's a guarantee.

KREMS GEHT AUF SENDUNG
KREMS GOES ON THE AIR

Wenn aus dem Gelände der Winzer Krems die Musik live über Ö1 und weitere europäische Radiostationen in die halbe Welt klingt, dann wird bei Glatt&Verkehrt aufgespielt. Wenn im Rahmen des donaufestivals Musik, Theater und Bildende Kunst hochaktuelle Themen aus künstlerischer Sicht interpretieren, dann berichtet Radio FM4 gemeinsam mit vielen weiteren Medien über Krems. Im Rahmen vom Osterfestival Imago Dei wird die Minoritenkirche ein Klangraum für zeitlose Kunst – und das in großer medialer Begleitung.

Krems braucht kein Theater- oder Konzerthaus, um renommierten Künstlerinnen und Künstlern die große Bühne zu bieten. Und die Gäste wissen, was sie erwartet. Sie nehmen die außergewöhnlichen Orte, eingebettet in die einzigartige Landschaft, mit Freude an und schätzen die Infrastruktur der Tourismusstadt. Echte Fans buchen Monate im Voraus die begehrten Tickets.

***When live music** is broadcast halfway round the world from Winzer Krems by Ö1 and other European radio stations, it's a performance at the Glatt&Verkehrt festival. When the topics of the day are given an artistic interpretation by music, drama and visual arts at the donaufestival, Radio FM 4 and many other media feature Krems in their reports. During the Imago Dei Easter festival the Minoritenkirche becomes a sound space for timeless art, accompanied by extensive media coverage.*

Krems has no need of a theatre or concert hall to provide distinguished artists with a suitably large stage. And the visitors know what to expect. They enthusiastically flock to the unconventional venues set amid unique scenery and appreciate the amenities provided by the tourist city. The real fans book the highly prized tickets months in advance.

oben: Musikfestival Glatt&Verkehrt | *above: Glatt&Verkehrt music festival*
rechts: Musikfestival Glatt&Verkehrt | *right: Glatt&Verkehrt music festival*

FILM
BAR
KULINARIUM

KINO UNTER STERNEN
MOVIES UNDER THE STARS

Alle Jahre wieder lädt das Kino im Kesselhaus zu Filmgenuss unter freiem Himmel. Und den Rest des Jahres gibt es neben vielen Filmen auch Konzerte und weitere Events im Kinosaal.

Every year *the cinema in the boiler house stages an open-air event for film buffs. During the rest of the year, other events are held there besides the many films and concerts.*

Kino im Kesselhaus | *Films in the Boiler House*

Nächste Seite: Zeitgenössische Kunst am Campus
next page: Contemporary art on the Campus

KUNST DEFINIERT DEN WEG
ART SHOWS THE WAY

Kunst im öffentlichen Raum ist wegweisender Teil der Kulturlandschaft des Landes Niederösterreich. In Krems verändern Kunstwerke nicht nur am Campus die Perspektiven.

Art in public places *is a pioneering part of the culture scene in Lower Austria. In Krems, artworks shift perspectives, and not just on the Campus.*

KULTUR UND BRAUCH
CULTURE AND CUSTOMS

Ein Haus für 270 europäische Regionen an der Steiner Donaulände bittet zu Musik, Tanz und Literatur und zum Diskurs. Ein Fachgeschäft für Kunsthandwerk und ergänzende kulinarische Erlebnisse runden das Angebot ab. Die Volkskultur Niederösterreich hat den Ort im Hotspot des Donautourismus bewusst gewählt und bietet ihren Gästen Traditionspflege auf höchstem Niveau.

In Krems und in der Region wird seit Generationen Kultur gemeinsam gepflegt und weitergegeben. Die städtische Musikschule fördert Talente, die Karriere machen. Die Kapellen und die Volkstanzgruppe haben kaum Nachwuchssorgen. Junge Literaten oder bildende Künstlerinnen und Künstler finden Räume für erste Schritte an die Öffentlichkeit.

Und die kunstinteressierten Kremserinnen und Kremser bleiben nicht auf der Strecke. Sie nehmen die abwechslungsreichen Angebote in den Kunsthäusern gerne an. Im Rahmen der Konzerte der Köchelgesellschaft sind einleitende Fachgespräche fixer Teil des Angebotes, an der Donau-Universität werden neue Formen der Kunstvermittlung gelehrt.

***A building** for 270 European regions invites people to music events, dance, literature and debate on Donaulände in Stein. A shop specialising in handicrafts and accompanying culinary delicacies complete the activities on offer. Volkskultur Niederösterreich consciously chose the town, a hotspot of tourism on the Danube, and offers visitors tradition cultivated to the highest standard.*

For generations, culture has been maintained and handed down in Krems and the region as a community activity. The municipal music school promotes talented children who become professionals. The bands and folk dance troupes have little difficulty attracting new members. Young writers and visual artists find places to introduce their work to the public.

And the art aficionados among the people of Krems are not backward in coming forward. They enthusiastically take part in the various activities at the art institutions. Introductory talks by experts are an integral part of the concerts staged by the Köchel Society, while at the Danube University new forms of education in art are taught.

RADIO

BÜHNE FREI!
LIVE ON STAGE

Ob auf der Bühne in der Musikschule, im Haus der Regionen, im Salzstadl oder im großen Konzertraum, in Krems finden sich Jung und Alt vor und auf der Bühne.

***On the stage** in the music school, in the Haus der Regionen, in the Salzstadl or the large auditorium: these are places in Krems where young and old take the stage or sit in front of it.*

Bühne im Hof der Winzer Krems
Stage in the courtyard of Winzer Krems

Nächste Seite (von links oben im Uhrzeigersinn)
next page (clockwise from top left)
Literaturhaus NÖ | *Lower Austrian Literaturhaus*
Minoritenkirche | *Minoritenkirche*
Artothek NÖ | *Lower Austrian Artothek*
Kunsthalle Krems | *Kunsthalle Krems*

Fixpunkte im Jahreskreislauf der Kulturfestivals sind: Osterfestival Imago Dei, Literatur und Wein, donaufestival, Open-Air-Kino Kesselhaus, Glatt&Verkehrt. Aus der Liste an international renommierten Ausstellungshäusern: Minoritenkirche, Kunsthalle Krems, Forum Frohner, Karikaturmuseum, Dominikanerkirche, Landesgalerie Niederösterreich (Eröffnung 2018).

***Regular items** in the annual festival calendar are: Imago Dei Easter Festival, Literatur und Wein, donaufestival, Kesselhaus open-air cinema, Glatt&Verkehrt. The list of internationally celebrated exhibition venues includes: Minoritenkirche, Kunsthalle Krems, Forum Frohner, Karikaturmuseum, Dominikanerkirche, Landesgalerie Niederösterreich (opening 2018).*

Exzellent gewirtschaftet, das gilt für viele Betriebe, die den Standort in der Donaumetropole oft seit Generationen schätzen. Ständige Investitionen der mittlerweile international tätigen Großbetriebe mit Sitz in Krems zeigen, dass der gemeinsame Weg stimmt. Auch die Kremser profitieren auf vielfältige Art, egal ob als Arbeitnehmer, ob als Unternehmer oder auch als Konsument. Bio-Produkte aus dem Waldviertel, gediegene Fachgeschäfte und innovative Industriebetriebe: Krems ist Feinkostladen, Fachhandel und Wirtschaftsmotor für die ganze Region.

Excellent management: This applies to many companies that appreciate the location on the Danube, as many have done for generations. Constant investment by large concerns that now operate globally from their headquarters in Krems shows that the path taken together is the right one. There are also many benefits for the people of Krems, be they employees, entrepreneurs or consumers. Organic products from the Waldviertel, elegant specialist stores and innovative industrial firms: Krems is the delicatessen, specialist retailer and economic motor of the entire region.

eigener
3,–
3,–
3,50
500 ml 16,–
100 ml 6,–

AUS DEM VOLLEN SCHÖPFEN
FROM THE HORN OF PLENTY

Frisch vom Markt, das ist kein leeres Versprechen. Schon im Mittelalter war Krems Feinkostladen für das Waldviertel. Damals waren am Hohen Markt die Fleisch- und Brotbänke ab dem frühen Morgen Zentren geschäftigen Feilschens. Und die Bauern der Region karrten Hühner und Eier aus dem Stall und erntefrisches Gemüse vom Feld in die Stadt.

Diese Gewohnheit ging nicht verloren, heute bringen die Bäuerinnen und Bauern zwar keine lebenden Hühner, jedenfalls aber drei Mal pro Woche ihre Produkte auf den Markt. Fische aus dem Waldviertel, appetitlich duftender Käse, je nach Saison Morcheln, Spargel oder Pilze, Salate und Gemüse. Beste Zutaten für ein gelungenes Fest daheim finden die Hausfrauen und Hobbyköche mittwochs und samstags am Pfarrplatz und freitags am Dreifaltigkeitsplatz. Sie freuen sich auf handgemachte Teigwaren und auf die Waldviertler Erdäpfel. Und sie schätzen es, dass es in Krems noch mehrere lokale Bäcker und Fleischhauer gibt, die Sonderwünsche ihrer Kunden zur vollen Zufriedenheit erfüllen.

Die Gaumenfreuden alleine würden nicht reichen. Die bunte Mischung aus edlen Textil- und Schuhgeschäften, aus Juwelieren und Optikern, aus selten gewordenen Fachläden für Eisenwaren, Elektronik und Porzellan, eine Glaserei und eine Buchbinderei ziehen Kunden aus der ganzen Region in die Stadt zum Einkaufen. Dass eine Rösterei selbst importierte und vor Ort geröstete Kaffeespezialitäten kreiert, das hat Tradition in Krems. Ein bestens sortierter Tee- und Gewürzladen und viele weitere Fachgeschäfte sind längst keine Geheimtipps mehr. Die Konditoren übertreffen einander mit Schöpfungen aus feinster Schokolade. Das legendäre Wachauer Laberl wird ofenfrisch angeboten. Die Produkte aus der Wachauer Marille – Marmelade und Schnaps – sind ein Verkaufshit. Samstags früh wird die Landstraße mit ihren Wirtshäusern, Restaurants, Bars und den behaglichen Cafés zur Flaniermeile für die Kremserinnen und Kremser.

Fresh from the market *is no empty promise. Krems was already supplying the Waldviertel with fine foods in the Middle Ages. In those days, the meat and bread benches on Hoher Markt were the scene of animated bargaining from the early morning. The region's farmers carted chickens and eggs from their henhouses and freshly picked vegetables from their fields into the town.*

This custom never died out: today, although they no longer have live poultry with them, the farmers bring their produce to market three times a week. Fish from the Waldviertel, delicious-smelling cheese, and morels, asparagus, mushrooms, lettuce and vegetables when they are in season. Housewives and keen cooks can find first-rate ingredients for a successful feast at home on Pfarrplatz on Wednesdays and Saturdays and on Dreifaltigkeitsplatz on Fridays. They look forward to home-made pasta and Waldviertel potatoes. And they appreciate the fact that Krems still has several local bakers and butchers who can meet any special wishes and provide exactly what they want.

But the tasty delicacies alone would not be enough. The motley assortment of high-class boutiques and shoe shops, jewellers and opticians, with specialists in hardware, electrical appliances and porcelain that are rare nowadays, plus a glazier and a bookbinder attract shoppers to the city from the whole region. That a roasting establishment creates coffee specialities it imports itself and roasts in the shop is a tradition in Krems. A tea and spice shop with a superb range of wares has long since ceased to be an insiders' tip, as have many other specialist stores. The confectioners outdo each other with their creations from the finest chocolate. The legendary Wachauer loaf is sold freshly baked. The jam and schnapps made from the Wachau apricot are hugely popular. On Saturday mornings, Landstraße with its inns, restaurants, bars and cosy cafés becomes a promenade for the people of Krems.

太陽飯店
China-Restaurant
JO-HAN CHIU
Coca-Cola
IM HOF
BUCH
SCHMIDL
PAPIER
Radiodoktor
novotny
RED ZAC
Steinecker
dm
SPAR
RENO

QUALITÄT IM ZENTRUM

QUALITY IN THE CENTRE

Ein Zwischenstopp beim lustvollen Einkaufsbummel durch die Innenstadt lohnt sich. Die Hausfassaden zeugen von den Leistungen der Händler seit Jahrhunderten.

A break *during the pleasurable shopping stroll round the city centre is well worth it. The buildings' facades bear witness to the accomplishments of tradesmen down the centuries.*

Obere Landstraße | *Obere Landstraße*

MEISTER AM WERK
MASTERS AT WORK

Althergebrachte Handwerkskunst wird in Krems gelebt. Mit Kreativität und technischer Meisterschaft arbeiten die Kremser Fachbetriebe für ihre Kunden. Die Volkskultur Niederösterreich bietet dazu erlesene Handwerksprodukte aus ganz Österreich.

***Traditional** arts and crafts are part of life in Krems. The specialist firms work for their customers with creativity and technical expertise. Volkskultur Niederösterreich offers exquisite handicraft products from all over Austria.*

ganz oben: Volkskultur Niederösterreich – Handwerk der Regionen | *top: Volkskultur Niederösterreich - Handwerk der Regionen*
oben: Buchbinderei Juriatti | *above: Juriatti the bookbinder's*
rechts: Schneiderei Gerda Gartler | *right: Gerda Gartler, seamstress*

GMUNDNER
Swarovski Elements - Stand 2012
Burgundy
Light Amethyst
Tanzanite
Amethyst
Purple Velvet
Montana
Sapphire
Light Sapphire
Light Turquoise
Peridot
Fern Green
Light Topaz
Jonquil
Topaz
Smoked Topaz
SCHRABACHER

AN DER SPITZE
AT THE TOP

Kremser Betriebe sind hoch spezialisiert. Restaurator Hadeyer etwa, der nicht nur vor Ort, in der Musterstadt der Denkmalpflege, sondern in ganz Niederösterreich und Wien gefragt ist.

Krems firms *are highly specialised. Restorer Hadeyer, for example, who is in great demand not only here in the model city of historic preservation, but all over Lower Austria and in Vienna.*

Arbeiten an der Stadtmauer | *Work on the city wall*

DIE SÜSSE BOTSCHAFT
THE SWEET AMBASSADOR

Die Wachauer Marille wurde vor rund 100 Jahren neben dem Wein zur kulinarischen Botschafterin der Region. Veredelt als Marmelade, Likör oder Edelbrand, wie etwa von der Privatdestillerie Hellerschmid – die Marille begeistert Gourmets.

Approximately 100 years ago, *the Wachau apricot joined wine as the region's culinary ambassador. Worked into jams, liqueurs or spirits, such as those made by the Hellerschmid distillery, the apricot delights gourmets.*

links: Geschäft am Steiner Tor | *left: Shop by the Steiner Tor*
ganz oben: Destillerie Hellerschmid | *top: Hellerschmid distillery*
oben: Edelbrände | *above: Spirits*

VOLL IM TREND
THE HEIGHT OF FASHION

Der Spannungsbogen vom Gestern bis zum Heute wird in den vielfältigen Angeboten der Innenstadt gehalten. Das Angebot stimmt in Krems.

The arc of suspense *between yesterday and today is maintained by the great diversity on offer in the city centre. What Krems offers meets the demand.*

Obere Landstraße | *Obere Landstraße*

ADLER APOTHEKE
seit 1526
ADLER APOTHEKE
KLIMESCH SCHUHE
Foto
Hartlauer
Optik
Wolford
ADLER OPTIK
BESTE BERATUNG

KREMSER BANK
ANK

SERVICE FÜRS LEBEN
SERVICE FOR LIFE

Große Industriebetriebe, hoch qualifizierte Handwerksbetriebe und unzählige weitere Unternehmen und Dienstleister schätzen den Standort. Die Grundlagen wurden über Generationen gelegt. Die Entwicklung wird von den lokalen Finanzdienstleistern professionell begleitet. Krems ist regionales Finanzzentrum. Die KREMSER BANK und Sparkassen AG zählt zu den größten Arbeitgebern und ist aktiver Förderer des wirtschaftlichen, sozialen, kulturellen und sportlichen Lebens in der Region.

Large industrial companies, *highly qualified craft enterprises and countless other firms and service providers appreciate the location. The foundations were laid over the course of several generations. Development is professionally supported by the local financial services providers. Krems is a regional centre of finance. KREMSER BANK und Sparkassen AG is one of the biggest employers and actively supports the economic, social, cultural and sporting life of the region.*

KREMSER BANK, Ringstraße | *KREMSER BANK, Ringstraße*

MARKTFÜHRER
MARKET LEADER

Die voestalpine am Kremser Hafen ist europäischer Marktführer in der Produktion von kaltgewalzten Stahlrohren und Stahlprofilen. Eine hochmoderne Lehrwerkstätte ist der Antrieb für viele Karrieren.

voestalpine *at Krems port is a European market leader in the production of cold rolled steel pipes and steel profiles. A state-of-the-art apprentice workshop is the springboard for many careers.*

DREHSCHEIBE DES HANDELS
COMMERCIAL HUB

Die Kräne definieren die Hafenanlage im Osten der Stadt und signalisieren, dass europaweit gehandelt wird. Der Kremser Hafen ist der viertgrößte in Österreich und wächst ständig.

Cranes *dominate the port facilities in the east of the city and show that trade is conducted with all of Europe. The port in Krems is the fourth largest in Austria, and constantly growing.*

brantner.com
brantner
CO2-minimiert
lärmreduziert
brantner
brantner
KS 344 BN
14
bücherei

FÜR UNSERE UMWELT
FOR OUR ENVIRONMENT

Vom Firmensitz Krems zu einem europäischen Marktführer, so kann man die Erfolgsstory der Brantner Gruppe auf den Punkt bringen. In 64 Niederlassungen in Europa und Asien leisten mehr als 2.500 Mitarbeiterinnen und Mitarbeiter in den Bereichen Entsorgung, Facility Services und Logistik mit innovativen Konzepten für die Wiederverwertung maßgebliche Beiträge zum Umweltschutz.

From the company headquarters in Krems *to a European market leader: that, in a nutshell, is the success story of the Brantner Group. In 64 branches in Europe and Asia, a workforce of over 2,500 makes a crucial contribution to environmental protection with its work in the fields of waste disposal, facility services and logistics with innovative concepts for recycling.*

Am Körnermarkt | *On Körnermarkt*

GEMEINSAM ZUM ERFOLG
ACHIEVING SUCCESS TOGETHER

Die Unternehmen haben in Krems optimale Partner in Lehre und Ausbildung. Sie finden ebenso die adäquaten Räume für ihre Forschungsvorhaben.

In Krems, *companies have the ideal partners for apprenticeships and training. They also find suitable premises for their research projects.*

ganz oben: Fresenius Medical Care | *top: Fresenius Medical Care*
oben: Industriezone Krems | *above: Krems industrial estate*
rechts: Werkshalle voestalpine Krems | *right: Workshop at voestalpine Krems*

Nächste Seite (von links oben im Uhrzeigersinn) | *next page (clockwise from top left)*
Donauhafen Krems | *Krems Danube port*
Buchbinderei Juriatti | *Juriatti the bookbinder's*
Werkhalle | *Workshop*
Am Steiner Tor | *By the Steiner Tor*

K64

Hochspezialisierte Handwerksbetriebe und dynamische Industrieunternehmen sind der sichtbare Beweis für die hohen Leistungen. Krems ist eine florierende Wirtschaftsstadt, auch wenn man es beim lustvollen Einkaufsbummel in der Innenstadt nicht gleich vermutet: Krems ist nicht nur eine Stadt des Einkaufs, sondern auch der Wirtschaft.

***Highly specialised craft enterprises** and dynamic industrial firms provide visible proof of the considerable achievements. Krems is a thriving centre of business and industry, even though this may not be immediately obvious on a leisurely shopping stroll through the city centre: Krems is not just a shopping city, but a commercial centre too.*

Fest verankert in der Stadt ist der Weinbau. Er formte schon vor mehr als tausend Jahren die Landschaft am Donaustrom und prägt bis heute das Stadtbild. Ob beim Heurigen oder in den Restaurants, ob auf den Kellergassenfesten oder auf internationalen Fachmessen, der Wein aus Krems ist begehrt. Beste landschaftliche Voraussetzungen und hervorragende Ausbildung der Winzer sind Grundlagen für die Erfolge. Die wein.genuss.krems in der Dominikanerkirche als Auftakt des wachau GOURMETfestivals ist ein guter Anlass, um alljährlich seine eigenen Favoriten zu küren.

Viniculture is deeply rooted in the city. Over a thousand years ago it was already shaping the landscape around the Danube, and still defines the city's character today. Wine from Krems is hugely popular, whether at a wine tavern or in the restaurants, at a wine cellar party or an international trade fair. Its success stems from the perfect conditions found in the area and the outstanding training that the winegrowers undergo. wein.genuss.krems, the curtain-raiser of the annual wachau GOURMETfestival in the Dominikanerkirche, is a good opportunity for wine-lovers to choose their favourites.

LETH
LOIMER
34

EIN PLATZ AN DER SONNE
A PLACE IN THE SUN

Der Wettlauf um die Weinbauflächen rund um Krems an der Donau begann schon im Mittelalter. Denn Boden und Klima passen hier. Waren zunächst die Vertreter der großen mitteleuropäischen Klöster im Vorteil, so sind es heute, nach den Klosteraufhebungen im 18. Jahrhundert, hoch qualifizierte Weinhauer, die den Markt erobert haben. Mittlerweile sind die Weine aus Krems und aus der Region rund um den Globus erfolgreich und gefragt.

Das beweist die gute Entscheidung der Vorfahren und zeigt die besondere Eignung der Landschaft rund um den jahrhundertealten Weinort. Die Weinstadt Krems liegt de facto am Schnittpunkt mehrerer Weinbaugebiete Niederösterreichs. Doch die perfekte Lage alleine würde nicht reichen, es bedarf des versierten Könnens und hohen Einsatzes der Winzerinnen und Winzer, um den Wein weltweit zu einem begehrten Spitzenprodukt zu machen.

Dass der Wein einst als wertvolles Handelsgut den Fortschritt der Stadt wesentlich beeinflusste, das ist bis heute unverändert. In kaum einer Stadt reichen die Weinberge bis unmittelbar ans Zentrum und prägen die Landschaft bis vor die Hörsäle der Hochschulen. Dass es in Krems die älteste noch aktive Hauerinnung Mitteleuropas gibt, dass das Weingut der Stadt 550 Jahre alt ist und dass die Wein- und Obstbauschule gleichzeitig eines der modernsten Kompetenzzentren in der Ausbildung der Winzerelite von morgen ist, das ist angesichts des Stellenwertes des Weinbaues in Krems nur konsequent.

Genießen kann man die Weine aus Krems bei den Heurigen und in den Vinotheken und Restaurants. Die Winzer laden alljährlich auf Weinfeste, zu Kellerführungen und in ihre Vinotheken. Und im Frühjahr gibt es die vom Fachmagazin Vinaria prämierten besten Weine des Landes in der Dominikanerkirche im Rahmen des wachau GOURMETfestivals zu verkosten.

The rush *to secure sites for wine-growing around Krems an der Donau began way back in the Middle Ages. Here, the soil and the climate are perfect. Initially it was those connected to the large medieval central European monasteries who were at an advantage, but today, following the dissolution of many monasteries in the 18th century, highly qualified winegrowers have taken over the market. Wines from Krems and the region are now successful and in demand the world over.*

This proves that the ancestors made the right decision and underlines the eminent suitability of the countryside around the centuries-old wine town of Krems, which actually lies at the intersection of several Lower Austrian wine-growing areas. However, its ideal location alone is not enough: the tremendous skill and efforts of the winegrowers are also needed to make the wine a globally sought-after, premium product.

Wine, as a valuable commodity, once played a key role in the city's development, and this still holds true today. Almost nowhere else do the vineyards sweep down to the very edge of the town centre or dominate the scenery right outside the university lecture theatres. Considering the importance of viniculture in Krems it is only logical that the oldest, still active winegrowers' guild in central Europe is in Krems, that the city's vineyard estate is 550 years old and that the wine- and fruit-growing school is among the most modern competence centres for training tomorrow's foremost winemakers.

Krems wines can be enjoyed at the wine taverns and in the wine shops and restaurants. Every year the winemakers organise wine fairs, cellar tours and visits to their shops. And in spring, the wines chosen by the trade journal Vinaria as the country's best can be tasted in the Dominikanerkirche during the wachau GOURMETfestival.

MIT WEITBLICK ZUM BESTSELLER
VISION MAKES A BESTSELLER

Die Kremser Hauerinnung besteht seit 1447. Dass sie die Winzer Krems gründete, die nunmehr in die ganze Welt exportiert, zeigt ihre Weitsicht.

The Krems Winegrowers' Guild *has existed since 1447. Their foundation of Winzer Krems, which now exports usw wine all over the world, proves their foresight.*

DER WEG ZUR SPITZE
THE ROAD TO THE TOP

Der optimale Umgang mit der einzigartigen Landschaft und dem Wein wird über Generationen weiterentwickelt. Der Kremser Wein wurde so zu einem Spitzenprodukt.

The ideal way *to manage the unique countryside and the wine has been constantly developed over generations. As a result, Krems wine became a premium product.*

Stadt Krems
KÖGL
Riesling

STADT MIT WEINGUT
CITY WITH A VINEYARD

550 Jahre machen das Stadtweingut von Krems zu einem der ältesten Weinproduzenten Europas. Das Lob der Experten und die Verkaufszahlen belegen den richtigen Weg.

Its 550 years *make the municipal vineyard in Krems one of the oldest wine producers in Europe. The accolades from experts and the sales figures show that the chosen path is right.*

links: historischer Weinkeller | *left: Historic wine cellar*
ganz oben: Stahltanks | *top: Steel tanks*
oben: Weingut Stadt Krems | *above: Stadt Krems vineyard*

HOCHKARÄTIGE BEWERTUNGEN
TOP MARKS

Viele Kremser Winzer haben sich nach wie vor ausschließlich dem Weinbau verschrieben und betreiben mit ihren Familien modernste Kellereien und Ab-Hof-Verkäufe. Die Väter sind ihre Vorbilder, Innovation und stete Verbesserung sind selbstverständlich. Sie präsentieren ihre Produkte stolz auf internationalen Fachmessen. Erfahrene Weinkenner schwärmen vom Ergebnis und stellen höchste Bewertungen aus. Der Wein aus dem Kremstal wird mit Recht immer mehr geschätzt, das bestätigt gleichermaßen die Fachpresse.

Der Grüne Veltliner hat in der Region um Krems seine eigentliche Heimat, er trat von hier aus seinen Siegeszug an. Doch nicht nur Veltliner und Rieslinge, auch seltenere Weißweinsorten wie Chardonnay, Sauvignon Blanc oder Muskateller und Rotweine aus der Region sind bei den Kennern inzwischen gefragt. Die Sektmanufaktur von Josef Dockner am Südufer der Donau ergänzt die Palette an Produkten rund um den Kremser Wein.

Many winegrowers *in Krems continue to devote themselves exclusively to viniculture, run state-of-the-art wine cellars with their families and sell their wine themselves. Their role models are their fathers, while innovation and constant improvement are taken for granted. They proudly present their products at international trade fairs. Experienced connoisseurs are fulsome in their praise of the results and give top marks. Wine from the Krems valley is gaining more and more admiration, and rightly so. This view is echoed by the trade press.*

The Grüner Veltliner grape has its true home in the region around Krems: it was here that its success story started. Besides Veltliners and Rieslings, rarer whites such as Chardonnay, Sauvignon Blanc and Muscatel, as well as reds from the region, are now in demand too. Josef Dockner's sekt factory on the south bank of the Danube adds to the range of products in the Krems wine collection.

oben: In den Weingärten | *above: In the vineyards*
rechts: Am Frauengrund | *right: On Frauengrund hill*

Josef
DOCKNER

NACH BESTER TRADITION
IN THE BEST TRADITION

In der Sektmanufaktur von Josef Dockner am Kremser Frauengrund gärt und reift der Sekt nach der Méthode traditionnelle in der Flasche. In sorgfältiger Handarbeit entsteht ein weiteres Spitzenprodukt der Winzerfamilie Dockner.

In Josef Dockner's sekt factory *on Frauengrund hill in Krems the sekt ferments and matures in the bottle according to the méthode traditionnelle. Made meticulously by hand, another high-class product from the Dockner family of winegrowers is completed.*

Sektmanufaktur Josef Dockner
Sektmanufaktur Josef Dockner

ERFAHRUNG BRINGT ERFOLG
SUCCESS THROUGH EXPERIENCE

Erfahrung und Wissen im Umgang mit der Natur, von Boden und Klima seit Generationen, Kenntnis neuester Technologien und stetiges Suchen nach Verbesserungen, das führt Winzer aus dem Kremstal wie Wolfgang Aigner aus Krems-Weinzierl zu ihren Leistungen, die auch honoriert werden: sie haben Weinkenner auf der ganzen Welt als Kunden.

***Experience and knowledge** of nature, the soil and the climate that go back generations, expertise in the latest technologies and a constant quest for improvements are behind the success of Krems valley winegrowers such as Wolfgang Aigner from Weinzierl in Krems whose customers include wine connoisseurs the world over.*

WISSEN, WIE ES GEHT
LEARNING THE ART

Weinmachen will gelernt sein. In Krems kann man es an der Wein- und Obstbauschule Krems von Grund auf lernen. Und in Kursen das Wissen ständig verfeinern und auf dem neuesten Stand halten.

Wine-making *must be learned. In Krems, the wine- and fruit-growing school teaches wine-makers everything they need to know. Courses help them to specialise and keep abreast of the latest developments.*

TPG

Als Stadt der guten Weißweine hat sich Krems vor allem dank des ausgezeichneten Grünen Veltliners und des beliebten Rieslings einen Namen gemacht. 320 Weinbaubetriebe produzieren den Kremser Wein. Mitnehmen kann man ihn in den Vinotheken und direkt bei 40 Heurigen, bei den Winzern ab Hof und auf den Kellergassenfesten.

***Krems' reputation** as a city of good white wines stems chiefly from the outstanding Grüner Veltliner and the popular Riesling. The Krems wines are produced by 320 wineries. They are on sale at the wine shops, at 40 wine taverns, direct from the wine-makers themselves and at the cellar parties.*

Genussmenschen haben es nicht leicht in Krems, denn es gibt viel zu entdecken. Und sie kommen auf ihre Rechnung. Kunst und Kultur, Erlebnis Donau und intakte Weinlandschaft, versteckte Fotowinkel und bekannte Motive, Kulinarik und Shoppen machen den speziellen Mix von Krems aus. Krems bietet, eingebettet in die herrliche Landschaft der Wachau, eine breite Palette an Angeboten für Kenner und Genießer – vom optimalen Quartier für alle Interessen über beste Gaumenfreuden bis zu bemerkenswert vielfältigen Sportmöglichkeiten.

Pleasure-seekers are spoilt for choice in Krems: there is so much to discover. And they certainly find something to savour. Art and culture, the Danube experience, unspoilt scenic vineyards, hidden photo opportunities and famous sights, dining and shopping make up Krems' exceptional mix. Nestling in the stunning Wachau landscape, Krems offers a wide range of activities for connoisseurs of all kinds, from accommodation fit for any purpose to superb delicacies and a remarkable variety of sports.

özKURULAR
Sinerji
FRISCHE QUALITÄT
UNVERÄUSSERLICHE LEIHSTEIGE

Dekor
%

ALLES FÜR DEN GAST
EVERYTHING FOR THE GUEST

Krems liegt in der Wachau. Damit ist schon Wesentliches zum Thema Tourismus gesagt, denn kaum eine Region Österreichs hat in den letzten Jahren eine derartig rasante Entwicklung zu verzeichnen, wie das einst verträumte Donautal zwischen Melk und Krems. Eine Fülle von saisonalen Events, vom Osterreigen bis zum Wachauer Advent, lädt alljährlich zu Konzerten, Ausstellungen und Kirchenführungen. Zeitgenössische Kunstwerke säumen den Weg und setzen neue Akzente.

Dass die Leistungen der Vergangenheit hochgehalten werden, das zieht jährlich hunderttausende Gäste in die Region. Stilvoll restaurierte Baudenkmäler mit jungem Leben und die einzigartige Naturlandschaft sind allgegenwärtig. Schifffahrt, Busse, Bahn und ein Leihradsystem sind gut vernetzt und ermöglichen sanfte Mobilität. Der Welterbesteig Wachau führt auf 180 km als Rundweg zum Wandern und Entschleunigen und trifft in der Innenstadt von Krems auf den Jakobsweg. Das verträumte Donautal, das einst als Filmkulisse europaweit bekannt wurde, ist heute ein auffallend jugendlicher Tourismusmagnet.

Und die Donaustadt als wertvoller Teil des Weltkulturerbes ist Ausgangs- und Endpunkt für viele Wachaubesuche. Die Schiffstation beim Welterbezentrum ist ein Hotspot des Tourismus, mit geballten Kulturangeboten wie selten in so kurzer Distanz. Die ganze Palette an kulinarischen Angeboten, vom Heurigen bis zur mit Hauben gekrönten Topgastronomie, ist vertreten. Egal ob Urlaub beim Winzer oder 4-Sterne-Betrieb, die Kremser Beherbergungsbetriebe garantieren entspannte Stunden.

Die Innenstadt ermöglicht Shoppen und Genuss, die Vororte punkten mit stimmungsvollen Verkostungen inmitten der außergewöhnlichen Weinlandschaft. Urbanes Stadtleben und als Kulturjuwel bekannte Erholungslandschaft in unmittelbarer Nähe, das trägt zum Reiz der Stadt bei. Kein Wunder, dass Krems als Tagungs- und Kongressstadt immer beliebter wird.

***Krems is in the Wachau region.** And that really says it all as far as tourism is concerned, because virtually no other region in Austria has undergone such a rapid development in recent years as the once sleepy Danube valley between Melk and Krems. A wealth of seasonal events, from the Osterreigen at Easter to the Wachau Advent, provide concerts, exhibitions and church tours every year. Contemporary artworks along the way offer new perspectives.*

Past accomplishments are cherished and upheld, which draws hundreds of thousands of visitors to the region every year. Tastefully restored historic buildings with young life and unique scenery are to be found everywhere. A well-coordinated system of travel by boat, bus, rail and hired cycle offers sustainable transport. The Welterbesteig Wachau is a 180-kilometre circular hiking trail ideal for a more leisurely pace. It joins the Way of St. James in Krems city centre. It is noticeable that the sleepy Danube valley, once famous throughout Europe as a film location, now attracts many young tourists.

And the city on the Danube, as a valuable part of the World Heritage Site, is the start and finish of many visits to the Wachau. The landing stage by the World Heritage Centre is a tourist hotspot with a concentration of cultural activities rarely found in such a small area. Examples of the entire range of eating establishments, from wine taverns to award-winning restaurants, can be found. The different types of accommodation in Krems, from farms to 4-star hotels, guarantee a relaxing stay.

The city centre offers shopping, dining and refreshment, while the outlying districts provide convivial tastings in a scenic vineyard setting. Stylish urban life and nearby countryside known as a cultural gem in which to unwind heighten the city's charm. It's no wonder that Krems is becoming more and more popular as a conference and congress centre.

Vorige Seite: Marktstand am Pfarrplatz | *previous page: Market stall on Pfarrplatz*

MOYOme, Obere Landstraße | *MOYOme, Obere Landstraße*

LEMONAID+

Rieslingbeuschl mit

FÜR GOURMETS
FOR GOURMETS

Vom Marktplatz zum legendären Gulasch sind es nur wenige Meter. Und davor, dazwischen und danach wird die Innenstadt ein Festplatz für Feinschmecker.

It is only a few metres *from the marketplace to the legendary goulash. And before, between and after, the city centre is an El Dorado for gourmets.*

Schwarze Kuchl, Untere Landstraße
Schwarze Kuchl, Untere Landstraße

MIT LUST UND LEIDENSCHAFT
PLEASURE AND PASSION

In der Weinstadt wird fleißig geröstet, geschäumt und mit Begeisterung Kaffee eingeschenkt. Das Kaffee Campus Krems im Zentrum der Innenstadt lebt den jungen Spirit der Stadt, der allgegenwärtig ist.

In the city of wine *there is much roasting, frothing and enthusiastic pouring of coffee. The Kaffee Campus Krems in the centre of the old town is filled with the city's young spirit which is felt everywhere.*

KAFFEE
CAMPUS
KREMS
Kaffee

SÜSSES UND PASTA
CONFECTIONERY AND PASTA

Cafés und Lokale als Treffpunkte der Studentinnen und Studenten entdeckt man zuhauf in Krems und in Stein. Und in hoher Qualität, wie die Stammgäste versichern.

Cafés and bars *where students meet are plentiful in Krems and Stein. And as the regulars will tell you, the quality is excellent.*

links: Stadtcafé Ulrich, Südtirolerplatz | *left: Stadtcafe Ulrich, Südtirolerplatz*
ganz oben: Café Wachau, Donaulände Stein | *top: Cafe Wachau, Donaulände, Stein*
oben: Ristorante Firenze, Schürerplatz | *above: Ristorante Firenze, Schürerplatz*

FESTE FEIERN
CELEBRATION TIME

Immer wieder laden Feste in die Innenstädte. Für kurze Zeit nur, vermutlich auch deswegen aber umso frequentierter. So wie der Leopoldimarkt am 15. November in Stein.

Celebrations *often provide a reason to visit the historic centres. The occasions may be brief, but all the more highly frequented. Like St. Leopold's Market on 15 November in Stein.*

Rathausplatz Stein | *Stein, Rathausplatz*

SPEZIELL FÜR DEN GAUMEN
SPECIALLY FOR THE TASTE BUDS

Seit dem Mittelalter ist Krems eine Stadt der Gaststuben und Wirtshäuser. Dass der süße Kremser Senf tatsächlich vor 500 Jahren hier erfunden wurde, das geriet etwas in Vergessenheit. Darum setzt Ulli Amon-Jell am Hohen Markt mitunter den Senfrostbraten auf ihre Speisekarte, denn die Gäste lieben die ausgezeichnete regionale Küche.

Die Gäste werden gut bedient in traditionellen Wirtshäusern, die sich der österreichischen Küche verschrieben haben und diese auf hohem Niveau verfeinern. Viele der Zutaten kommen aus der näheren Umgebung, das Waldviertel garantiert frischeste Produkte.

In der Universitätsstadt hat sich in den letzten Jahren auch eine junge Gastroszene erfolgreich etabliert. Mit internationaler Speisekarte, egal ob italienisch, griechisch oder asiatisch. Die meisten auf dem hohen Niveau, das die Gäste von Krems inzwischen erwarten.

Die Kaffeehauskultur wird gelebt und die Konditoren kreieren mit Meisterschaft täglich frühmorgens in den Backstuben ihre begehrten süßen Verführun-

Krems has been home *to many inns and restaurants ever since the Middle Ages. Today, few people realise that the sweet Kremser mustard really was invented here 500 years ago. That is why Ulli Amon-Jell sometimes puts a mustard roast on her menu on Hoher Markt since guests love her superb local dishes.*

Guests are well catered for in traditional restaurants that have specialised in Austrian fare to which they add their own deft touches. Many of the ingredients come from the surrounding area. The Waldviertel guarantees the freshest of produce.

In recent years, the university town has also seen the rise of a successful young catering scene. With international menus, from Italian and Greek to Asian. Most to the high standards that visitors to Krems have come to expect.

The coffee shop culture is alive and well, and early each day the confectioners expertly create their coveted sweet temptations in their bakeries. And of course the wine tavern culture is venerated, with home-made food and selected wines from their own cellars.

GASTHAUS JELL

DOMÄNE
WACHAU

BIER TRIFFT WEIN
BEER MEETS WINE

Dass das 2Stein auch einen stilvollen Weinkeller in Stein hat, das ist ein Geheimtipp. Er verrät, warum die Biergreißlerei im Schmid's beim Steinertor auch erlesene Weinspezialitäten bietet.

Only the initiated *know that 2Stein also has a stylish wine cellar in Stein. It explains why the beer store in Schmid's beim Steinertor also offers vintage wine specialities.*

HIP IST GUT
HIP IS GOOD

Überzeugte Fans hat das 2Stein als Flaggschiff der lebendigen, urbanen Lokalszene rund um den Campus viele. Küche, Service und Ambiente stimmen einfach.

As the flagship *of the vibrant, urbane bars and restaurants around the Campus, 2Stein has many ardent fans. The food, service and atmosphere are just perfect.*

2Stein, Dr.-Karl-Dorrek-Straße | *2Stein, Dr. Karl Dorrekstraße*

TREFFPUNKT KLOSTER UND
THE PLACE TO MEET: KLOSTER UND

Das ehemalige Kapuzinerkloster ist heute Eventlocation und Gourmetlokal. Von der stilvollen Hochzeit über exklusive Seminare und Firmenveranstaltungen bis zum harmonischen Abendessen mit Freunden im Haubenrestaurant LATE bietet es Genuss, Lifestyle und Kultur auf höchstem Niveau.

***Today, the former Capuchin monastery** is an event location and gourmet restaurant. From stylish weddings to exclusive seminars and corporate events to convivial evening meals with friends in the award-winning LATE restaurant it offers real pleasure, lifestyle and culture of the very highest standard.*

ganz oben: zeitgenössische Kunst im Kloster UND | *top: Contemporary Art in Kloster UND*
oben: Restaurant LATE | *above: LATE restaurant*
rechts: barockes Deckenfresko von Daniel Gran | *right: Baroque ceiling fresco by Daniel Gran*

FRISCH AUF DER GASSE
FRESH ON THE STREET

Die regionale Küche lebt in den Wirtshäusern hoch. Aber auch bei Steckerlfischen und Feuerflecken – auf den Kellergassenfesten bei den Winzern persönlich.

Regional cuisine *is celebrated in the restaurants. But also with skewered fish and "Feuerflecken" pita bread at cellar parties held by the winegrowers themselves.*

Kellergassenfest Thallern | *Thallern cellar party*

arte
Hotel Krems
www.arte-hotel.at
garage
ALEXANDRA
STYLING
CAFE
FASHION
Es tut gut - gut auszusehen...

WIR KOMMEN WIEDER
WE'LL BE BACK

300.000 Likes in Form von jährlichen Nächtigungen, das macht Krems zu einer Tourismusstadt, die mit der Region Wachau in den Rankings inzwischen eine der bekanntesten Destinationen Österreichs ist. Und das verpflichtet. Hoher Komfort, hervorragende Bedienung und ständige Innovationen zum Wohle der Gäste sind die Erfolgskriterien. Egal ob am Winzerhof oder in der 4-Sterne-Kategorie, die Kunden und ihre Wünsche stehen im Mittelpunkt und sie empfehlen gerne ihr Urlaubsquartier ihren Freunden und Bekannten weiter.

Kunst- und Kulturfreunde, Natur- und Outdoorfans, Gourmets und Weinfreunde, Studenten und Handelsreisende, Vortragende und Tagungsteilnehmer – alle finden das passende Angebot und stellen fest, dass die Zeit zu kurz war, um Krems wirklich kennenzulernen. Sie beginnen eine Beziehung ohne Ablaufdatum und freuen sich auf den nächsten Anlass, in Krems ein Zimmer zu buchen.

***300,000 likes** per year in the form of overnight stays make Krems a tourist city that has now joined the Wachau region in the rankings as one of Austria's best-known destinations. And that entails renewed efforts. A high level of comfort, outstanding service and constant innovation for the benefit of the guests are the success factors. Whether the accommodation is a vineyard or in the 4-star category, the focus is on the guests and their wishes, and visitors are happy to recommend their hosts to friends and family.*

Art and culture buffs, fans of nature and the great outdoors, gourmets and wine-lovers, students and travelling salesmen, speakers and conference delegates: they all find suitable accommodation and realise that their stay was too short to really get to know Krems. They begin a relationship with no expiry date and look forward to the next time they have cause to book a room in Krems.

DESIGN AUF STERNENIVEAU
STAR-STANDARD DESIGN

Trendiges Design und großzügige Zimmer, unmittelbar am Universitätscampus gelegen, 15 Minuten zur Innenstadt – damit punktet das arte Hotel Krems 365 Tage im Jahr bei seinen Gästen.

A trendy design *and spacious rooms, located right by the university campus, 15 minutes to the town centre: those are the plus points of the arte Hotel Krems for its guests 365 days a year.*

arte Hotel Krems, Dr.-Karl-Dorrek-Straße | *arte Hotel Krems, Dr. Karl Dorrekstraße*

MIT BEGEISTERUNG
WITH HEART AND SOUL

Gastgeber aus Leidenschaft. Das sind die Kremser Familienbetriebe, die seit Generationen persönliches Service mit modernstem Komfort verbinden.

Hosts with a passion. *These are the family businesses in Krems that have combined personal service with the latest in comfort for generations.*

ganz oben: Küche Gasthaus Jell, Hoher Markt | *top: The kitchen of Gasthaus Jell, Hoher Markt*
oben: Gaststube Gasthaus Jell | *above: Inside Gasthaus Jell*
rechts: Hotel Unter den Linden, Schillerstraße | *right: Hotel Unter den Linden, Schillerstraße*

Nächste Seite (von links oben im Uhrzeigersinn) | *next page (clockwise from top left)*
Café Raimitz, Bahnhofplatz | *Cafe Raimitz, Bahnhofplatz*
LATE im Kloster UND | *LATE im Kloster UND*
Woracziczky, Am Pfarrplatz | *Woracziczky, Am Pfarrplatz*
Am Wachauer Volksfest | *The Wachauer Volksfest*

den Linden

Beim Welterbezentrum in Stein treffen sich von der Marillenblüte bis zur Weinlese die geballten Touristenströme. Krems ist mit der Wachau eine der bekanntesten Destinationen Österreichs. Neben geballter Kunst und Kultur hat Krems im Jahreskreislauf viel zu bieten, etwa das wachau GOURMETfestival, das Wachauer Volksfest und den Wachaumarathon.

At the World Heritage Centre *in Stein tourists flock from apricot blossom time to the grape harvest. Along with the Wachau region, Krems is one of Austria's best-known destinations. Besides a high concentration of art and culture, Krems has much to offer all year round, such as the wachau GOURMETfestival, the Wachauer Volksfest and the Wachau Marathon.*

Hier möchte ich bleiben, das stellen viele Gäste immer häufiger fest. Denn heute ist Krems ein Ort zum Wohlfühlen und zum Verweilen. Als zentraler Ort einer Region unweit der Bundeshauptstadt ist die Stadt an der Donau längst nicht mehr die verträumte und idyllische Wein- und Tourismusstadt, sondern bietet erfrischend neue, urbane Facetten. So wurde sie zu einem gelungenen Beispiel für eine dynamische und attraktive Kommune, die sich mit Elan den aktuellen Herausforderungen stellt und hohe Lebensqualität bietet.

"I'd like to stay here." That is what many guests say, and increasingly often. Because Krems today is a place to feel at ease and to spend time. As the centre of a region, and not far from the Austrian capital, the city on the Danube has long since ceased to be a sleepy and idyllic city of wine and tourism and today offers refreshingly new, urbane facets. It has become a successful example of a dynamic and attractive municipality that enthusiastically meets today's challenges and offers a high quality of life.

MOBIL UND NAHELIEGEND
MOBILE AND NEARBY

Eine Erfolgsgeschichte über tausend Jahre bis ins Heute zu führen, das ist eine gewaltige Herausforderung. Und sie ist zu bewältigen. Das beweist das klare Ergebnis aktueller Umfragen und Rankings unter den österreichischen Städten, die die Donaustadt immer wieder im Spitzenfeld einreihen. Krems ist eben eine authentische Stadt mit einem Charakter, der sich durch Jahrhunderte geformt hat und der unverwechselbar ist. Er prägt das Stadtbild und die Bewohner und er färbt auf die Gäste ab.

Es sind viele Bausteine, die sich zum Wohle der Bewohner zusammenfügen. Krems ist eine Stadt, in der es sich gut wohnen lässt, eine Stadt, in der man Bildung, Arbeit und Freizeit optimal verbinden kann. Neue Urbanität und eine intakte Landschaft als Lebensgrundlagen verbinden sich in einer Symbiose, die mittlerweile Studierende aus der ganzen Welt anzieht. Die Infrastruktur passt, die meisten Einrichtungen und Angebote sind fußläufig erreichbar, obgleich manchmal der Eindruck entsteht, dass die Kremser oft und gerne das Auto nutzen. Selbst in die Kärntnerstraße nach Wien kommt man bequem und stressfrei mit der Bahn in 90 Minuten. Doch shoppen kann man genauso in Krems und das in hoher Güte. Die hochfrequentierte Fußgängerzone der Landstraße ist der tägliche Beweis dafür.

Im Bildungsbereich und bei den Kulturangeboten kann kaum eine Stadt einen so rasanten Anstieg verzeichnen, wie Krems an der Donau in der jüngsten Vergangenheit. Die örtliche Klinik ist nun Partner der Universität, eine der größten Wohnbaugesellschaften des Landes hat hier ihre Zentrale – das sind nur einige Beispiele für die hohe Qualität der zahlreichen Angebote vor Ort. Lehrer, Forscher und Studenten, Wirtschaftsbosse und Handwerker, Gourmets und Freizeitköche, Kaffeegenießer, Kunstfreunde und Freizeitsportler, Naturmenschen und Stadtmenschen, Familien und Singles, für alle gibt es die passenden Angebote in nächster Nähe. Zudem ist Krems nicht zuletzt eine soziale Stadt, die das soziale Miteinander organisiert.

Transferring *a thousand-year success story to the modern day is a huge challenge. But it can be done. This is proved by the clear results of recent surveys and rankings of Austrian towns which repeatedly put the city on the Danube among the leaders. Krems is simply an authentic town with a character formed over the course of centuries that is quite unmistakable. It defines the town and its inhabitants and leaves its mark on visitors.*

There are many components that combine to the benefit of the inhabitants. Krems is a desirable place to live, a city where education, work and leisure can be perfectly combined. New urbanity and unspoilt scenery form the foundations of daily life and combine in a symbiosis that now attracts students from all over the world. The infrastructure meets today's needs and most amenities can be reached on foot although it sometimes seems that the people of Krems prefer to drive everywhere. By train it is even possible to get to Kärntnerstraße in Vienna in 90 minutes, in comfort and with no stress. But shopping is also possible in Krems, and to high standards too, as the busy pedestrian zone, Landstraße, proves every day.

In the fields of education and culture, virtually no other town has undergone such rapid expansion in the recent past as Krems an der Donau. The city's clinic is now a partner of the university and one of Austria's biggest residential property development companies has its head offices here. These are just a few examples of the superior quality of the many local activities. Teachers, researchers and students, company bosses and craftsmen, gourmets and amateur cooks, coffee-lovers, art aficionados and recreational athletes, country folk and townies, families and singletons: all find the activities and amenities they need on their doorstep. Last but not least, Krems is a social city that organises community life.

Vorige Seite: Blick nach Osten | *previous page: The view eastward*

Bahnhof Krems | *Krems railway station*

Nächste Seite: Stadtreinigung am Dreifaltigkeitsplatz | *next page: Keeping the town tidy, Dreifaltigkeitsplatz*

Krems / Donau
Bahnhofsplatz
2-3 und 11
21
N
VOR

GEMEINSAM GESTALTEN
PULLING TOGETHER

Urbanes Leben braucht Räume für Begegnung und Kommunikation. Und intensive Pflege und Service. Die Mitarbeiter der Stadt sind dafür von früh bis spät im Einsatz.

Urban life *needs spaces to meet and communicate. As well as intensive service and maintenance. The municipal workforce takes care of it from dawn to dusk.*

FROM AN EARLY AGE

Die Kleinsten sind die Größten, wenn es um ihre Ansprüche und um ihre Zukunft geht. Krems bedeutet Abwechslung und Geborgenheit in stimmiger Umgebung.

***When it comes to** their needs and their future, the smallest of us are the greatest. Krems stands for variety and security in harmonious surroundings.*

links: International School | *left: International School*
oben: Stadtbücherei und Mediathek | *above: The municipal library and media library*

24 STUNDEN ONLINE
ONLINE ROUND THE CLOCK

Egal ob sorgsamer Umgang mit der Umwelt, optimale Betreuung für Jung und Alt, Sauberkeit und Sicherheit oder einfach das Leihrad als Nextbike ums Eck – es ist vorgesorgt. Und das Tag und Nacht: der Rettungshubschrauber in Krems-Gneixendorf hat seit 2017 als erster in Österreich Nachtflugdienst aufgenommen.

Whether it's careful use *of natural resources, the best possible care for young and old, cleanliness and safety or simply a hire bike round the corner – it's all in place. Night and day. In 2017, the rescue helicopter in Gneixendorf, Krems, became the first in Austria to fly night-time missions.*

Flugplatz Krems-Gneixendorf | *Gneixendorf airfield, Krems*

UNIQA
heliair
NOTRUF 144
ÖAMTC
Christophorus 2
BERGRETTUNGSDIENST ÖSTERREICH
ÖSTERREICHISCHES ROTES KREUZ

IHRE
NEUEN
TRAUM-
SCHUHE.

VOR DER HAUSTÜRE
ON THE DOORSTEP

Die Innenstadt bietet kurze Wege zu Arzt und Apotheke, zum Standesamt und zum Notar und zum Shoppen und Genießen. Wohlfühlen liegt im Zentrum.

In the city centre, *doctors and chemists, the registry office and solicitor, shops, bars and restaurants are never far away. Well-being is central!*

VORBILDLICHES WOHNEN
EXEMPLARY HOUSING

Die Gozzoburg am Hohen Markt war im 13. Jahrhundert einer der modernsten bürgerlichen Wohnpaläste Mitteleuropas. Wohnen in der Stadt war damals schon ein hohes Ziel. Ein Blick hinter die Fassaden der Stadthäuser zeigt schattige Innenhöfe und hochwertige Ausstattung. Neben prachtvollen Villenbauten aus der Gründerzeit stehen in Krems beispielgebende Architekturlösungen von heute.

Um 1900 setzte die Tabakindustrie mit ihren Arbeiterwohnungen neue Maßstäbe für soziales Wohnen in Stein. Wenige Jahrzehnte später entstand in „Lerchenfeld" eine Mustersiedlung für Arbeiterfamilien aus der Stahlindustrie. Der wesentliche Träger sozialer Wohnbauvorhaben ist seither die GEDESAG, die inzwischen in ganz Niederösterreich Miet- und Eigentumswohnungen sowie Reihenhäuser errichtet und verwaltet. Wohnangebote für Jungfamilien und ein Haus für betreutes Wohnen sowie die sorgfältige Instandsetzung historisch wertvoller Bausubstanz zeigen ebenso wie die einfühlsame Nachverdichtung am „Hundssteig" ihre reiche Erfahrung und zukunftsweisenden Schritte.

In the 13th century, *the Gozzoburg on Hoher Markt was one of the most modern residential palaces for non-nobles in central Europe. Even at that time, residing in the town was deemed desirable. A look behind the facades of the townhouses reveals shady courtyards and opulent furnishings. Magnificent villas from the Gründerzeit are now joined by groundbreaking, contemporary architectural solutions.*

In around 1900, the tobacco industry set new standards in low-cost housing with accommodation for employees in Stein. A few decades later, a model estate for the families of steelworkers was built in "Lerchenfeld". Since then, GEDESAG has been the most important low-cost residential property developer, and now builds and administers rented and owner-occupied flats and terraced houses all over Lower Austria. Housing for young families and a residential care home plus the careful restoration of buildings of historic value underline the company's great experience and forward-thinking strategy, as does the sensitive addition of housing to existing stock on "Hundssteig".

Schon vor über 700 Jahren schätzten die Bewohner die zentralen und doch ruhigen Lagen mit besonderem Ausblick als Orte fürs Wohnen.

***As early as 700 years ago** the townsfolk appreciated the centrally located yet quiet locations with the stunning views as places to live.*

AUFGEWECKT UND ATTRAKTIV
ASTUTE AND ATTRACTIVE

In Krems wurden und werden historische Wohnbauten musterhaft und beispielgebend für modernste Bedürfnisse revitalisiert. Die alten Adressen sind wieder in.

In Krems *historic houses have been, and still are, revitalised for today's needs in exemplary and pioneering fashion. The old addresses are back in fashion.*

links: Am Frauenberg | *left: On Frauenberg*
ganz oben: Dr.-Karl-Dorrek-Straße | *top: Dr. Karl Dorrekstraße*
oben: Göttweigerhof | *above: Göttweigerhof*

STADT UND LAND TOWN AND COUNTRY

Es ist ein aktueller Trend: das Leben in der Stadt soll auch ein Leben in und mit der Natur ermöglichen. Da wird der Uferweg am Kremsfluss ebenso wie die Donaupromenade zur Laufstrecke, wo man sich auf den Wachaumarathon vorbereitet. Rugbyspieler kämpfen am Ausportplatz um den Ball, Fußballer trainieren auf den Hobbysportplätzen und werden Fans der größeren Clubs. Die Parkanlagen werden Freizeitoasen für Groß und Klein.

Ob in Vereinen oder lieber alleine, Sportangebote gibt es in und um Krems für fast alle Sportarten, von der Kletterwand bis zum Fallschirmspringen. Das Rudern darf nicht fehlen, denn immerhin stellte Krems einst einen Olympiasieger im Rudersport.

***It's a trend of the moment:** living in town should also make a life in and with the countryside possible. Accordingly, the path alongside the river Krems and the Danube promenade become a running route on which to prepare for the Wachau Marathon. Rugby players tussle for the ball on the Ausportplatz, footballers train on the recreation grounds and become fans of the bigger clubs. The parks become oases of relaxation for people of all ages.*

In and around Krems virtually every sport is available, from climbing walls to parachute jumping, as a club member or alone. And rowing is a must: after all, there was once an Olympic gold medallist in rowing from Krems.

Steiner Ruder Club | *Stein Rowing Club*

steiner-ruder-club.at
STEINER R.C

GEMEINSAM VORAN
FORWARDS TOGETHER

KEIN KUNSTSTÜCK
EASY DOES IT

Der Handballverein UHK spielt in der obersten Liga um den Titel, die Fechtunion stellt Staatsmeister. Ob im Verein oder für sich alleine, jeder findet sein Angebot.

The UHK handball club *plays in the top division, while the fencing club includes the national champion. Whether in a club or alone, everyone finds a suitable sport.*

Sporthalle Krems | *Krems sports hall*

Nächste Seite: Skaterbahn in der Mitterau | *Next page: Mitterau skate park*

Platz für die Jugend, Spaß haben und die Natur genießen, ob an der Donau, in den Auen oder gleich neben der Wohnung. Räume gibt es genug, dafür sorgt die Stadt seit Jahren.

Room for the young, *having fun and enjoying the countryside – on the Danube, in the water meadows or right next to your home. For many years, the city has made sure there is enough room.*

RÄUME ZUR ERHOLUNG
SPACE TO UNWIND

Der historische Stadtpark ist auch dank der Privatstiftung Sparkasse Krems als finanzieller Unterstützer für die Restaurierung von Pavillon und Brunnen ein geschätzter Platz zur Erholung mitten in der Stadt.

The historic Stadtpark *is a popular spot to relax in the middle of the city, in part thanks to the Sparkasse Krems, the private foundation that gave funds to restore the pavilion and the fountain.*

THURNER

FREUNDE TREFFEN
MEETING FRIENDS

Die Kremser verstehen es, gemeinsam zu feiern. Das Wachauer Volksfest als eines der ältesten und größten des Landes lädt alle zwei Jahre in den Stadtpark zu Spaß und Geselligkeit unter dem Sternenhimmel. Die besten Weine der Region, ausgezeichnete Bierspezialitäten und kulinarische Schmankerl gehören dazu.

The people of Krems *know how to have a good time together. The Wachauer Volksfest is among the oldest and biggest fairs in the country, and every other year it offers fun and socialising under the stars in the Stadtpark. The region's best wines, superb speciality beers and culinary delicacies are essential ingredients.*

Wachauer Volksfest | *Wachauer Volksfest*

Nächste Seite: Bahnhofplatz Krems
next page: Krems Bahnhofplatz

MITEINANDER GESTALTEN
COLLECTIVE CREATIVITY

Der Bahnhofplatz wurde 1999 zu einem attraktiven Stadtraum, wobei die Lichtskulptur vom Künstler Michelangelo Pistoletto mit den Kremsern gemeinsam entworfen wurde.

***Bahnhofplatz** was turned into an attractive space in 1999, with the light sculpture being designed by the artist Michelangelo Pistoletto in conjunction with the citizens of Krems.*

ALT UND JUNG
OLD AND YOUNG

Die gelebte Mischung von Jung und Alt macht den besonderen Reiz von Krems aus. Behutsame Revitalisierung auf der Höhe der Zeit ist das Erfolgsrezept.

The unique charm *of Krems stems from the active amalgamation of young and old. Careful revitalisation in tune with the times is the recipe for success.*

Forum Frohner, Minoritenplatz | *Forum Frohner, Minoritenplatz*

Nächste Seite (von links oben im Uhrzeigersinn)
next page (clockwise from top left)
Donauschiff | *Danube barge*
Campus Krems | *Campus Krems*
Fußgängerzone | *Pedestrian zone*
Dominikanerkloster/Innenhof
Dominican monastery courtyard

forum
frohner
ernst krenek
forum
MEHR
SEHEN
LANGE
NACHT
SA | 1. OKT

Den Spagat zwischen Tradition und Moderne schaffen nicht viele Städte. Krems jedoch lebt die Kultur des Wandels. Als Stadt der kurzen Distanzen bietet sie im Weltkulturerbe Wachau ideale Voraussetzungen, um Lebensträume zu erfüllen. Egal ob zum Lernen, ob als Arbeitsplatz oder als Erholungsraum – Krems schafft Zukunft.

Not many cities *succeed in combining traditions and the modern age. But Krems embraces the culture of change. As a city of short distances it offers the ideal conditions to make lifelong dreams come true in the World Heritage Site that is the Wachau. Whether for learning, working or relaxing – Krems creates the future.*